# *Praise for* Footn

"Julie Lyles Carr helps us explore those who showed up faithfully and fulfilled their assignment but never found their way to the spotlight. It's a celebration of faithfulness. I love how interactive this study is and how beautifully deep it is."

—**Suzanne Eller**, cohost of *More Than Small Talk* podcast, best-selling author and communicator, founder of Living Free Together

"If you wonder if your ordinary life will have an impact on the world for Jesus, this Bible study will encourage you that no matter what your sphere of influence looks like, you have the potential to shine brightly for God."

—**Susie Davis**, cofounder of Austin Christian Fellowship, speaker, and author of *Dear Daughters: Love Letters to the Next Generation* and numerous other titles

"Abraham, Isaac, and Jacob; Peter, Paul, and Mary (not the folk singers)—these major players in the Bible are the topics of many Sunday morning messages, but often they leave us feeling ordinary and insignificant. In *Footnotes*, Julie Lyles Carr draws our attention to several bit players in the biblical narrative and masterfully draws out the significance of their stories. She reminds us that no role is too small, which means our small roles matter in a big way."

—**Lynn Marie Cherry**, pastor, speaker, and author of *Keep Walking: 40 Days to Hope and Freedom After Betrayal*

# footnotes*

*Major Lessons from Minor Bible Characters

JULIE LYLES CARR

**Footnotes**
Major Lessons from Minor Bible Characters

ISBN 978-1-5018-8854-0

19 20 21 22 23 24 25 26 27 28 — 10 9 8 7 6 5 4 3 2 1
MANUFACTURED IN THE UNITED STATES OF AMERICA

# Contents

# About the Author

Julie Lyles Carr is an author, speaker, broadcaster, and consultant who serves as the Pastor of LifeWomen Women's Ministry at her home church of LifeAustin in Austin, Texas. With degrees in psychology and English literature, she began her career in radio and television and continues in the broadcast and voice-over arena, including her work as an audiobook narrator. She founded the nonprofit Legacy of Hope, which today, through its 2dance2dream program, is dedicated to serving families with children with special needs. She is the author of *Raising an Original* and speaks regularly in both church and business settings. Her popular podcast, The Modern Motherhood Podcast, has welcomed guests such as Beth Moore, Priscilla Shirer, Bob Goff, and Max Lucado. Julie and her husband, Michael, are the parents of eight children, ranging in age from twelve to twenty-eight. You can find out more about Julie, her work, and her family life at julielylescarr.com.

Follow Julie:

   @JulieLylesCarr

   @julielylescarr

   @julielylescarr

Blog   julielylescarr.com (check here for event dates and booking information)

# Introduction

We hear a lot about the "big" names in the Bible. *Moses. Mary. Paul.* But what about those who are only mentioned in passing, or whose names aren't even known? What might they have to teach us about the faith journey?

*Footnotes* is a unique four-week study that introduces us to four invidivuals who make brief appearances in the Bible, just footnotes in the biblical story. They may be easy to overlook, but what we'll learn is that the impact of their lives should not be underestimated. Together we will be inspired by the backstories of these biblical figures, who show us that even minor players can teach major lessons.

## Getting Started

For this four-week study experience you will need this workbook, which includes personal lessons for each week, plus the corresponding video segments that are available for each lesson. We've also included Group Session Guides, which offer a road map you can use as you follow along or facilitate the session (more on that below).

## *Your Personal Study*

Each week consists of three sections or lessons for personal study. You might choose to do one lesson a day—whether three days in a row, every other day, or whenever you can find the time during your week. Or you might prefer to complete all three lessons over a couple of days or even in one sitting, depending on your schedule. Let your calendar and the Holy Spirit lead you to the routine or plan that's best for you.

Completing the lessons each week will help prepare you for the discussion and activities of the group session, but if you are unable to finish the lessons before the group session, don't let that keep you from showing up, listening, and participating. You will still be able to gain rich insights from the video and discussion—and bless the others in your group just by being present and contributing.

Though it is recommended that you complete this study with a group for the benefit of shared insights, support, and encouragement, a self-guided study is also possible.

### Meeting with a Group

When studying with a group, you'll gather each week to watch a video, discuss what you're learning, and pray together. The Group Session Guides, which provide options for both a 60-minute and a 90-minute session, include discussion questions, activities, prayer prompts, and a place for taking notes from the video segment. You'll find the outline for each session at the end of the personal lessons for that week.

If you're the facilitator or leader of your group, you'll want to check out the additional Leader Helps at the back of this book. Ideally, group members should complete the first week of lessons before your first group session, so that you may watch and discuss both the video and the workbook content in one session. However, feel free to adapt the study as you wish to meet the needs of your particular group.

Whether or not your group watches the video, the questions and activities will guide you in sharing your thoughts and making personal application as you seek to discover how God is speaking to you and where He is leading each of you on your faith journey.

### A Final Word

As we make this journey together, I encourage you to embrace your curiosity and prepare to be surprised by these unsuspecting "Footnotes" in the biblical story. In their own unique ways, each of these characters played a significant role in God's kingdom work, just as each of us does as well. My prayer is that you will come to realize as never before just how special, unique, and needed you are in God's great story.

*Julie*

# Week 1

## *Tychicus*

### *The Bridge*

---

# 1

---

*Let's build a bridge, take us across*
*Hand in hand, climbin' higher and higher*

"Let's Build a Bridge," by Billy Simon,
Robert B. Farrell, Tommy L. Sims

## Bridging Ages and Stages

It happened like clockwork when I was a kid. Every day at five-thirty p.m., dinner was on the table. It appeared magically, piping hot, nutritionally balanced, and budget friendly. We'd circle up at the table, pray over the meal, and dig in. We would eat, chat, and then my brothers and I would head for homework or the television.

Somehow, miraculously, the kitchen soon after returned to a tidy and clean state, the remaining leftovers of the meal left on a plate and covered with a protective sheet of plastic wrap in case pre-bedtime hunger called. Otherwise, the leftovers plate somehow made its way to the fridge. *Tick tock.*

Like I said, this phenonemon happened every day like clockwork—until I went to college. And then, something remarkable happened. While I was living on my own, dinner no longer just showed up. Groceries weren't automatically stocked in my kitchen. The pot with the charred macaroni didn't mysteriously get cleaned up during the night.

What was the difference? My mom.

My mom had been the bridge to those family meals, that organized kitchen, that dinnertime connection. She had gone about it relatively unnoticed and probably somewhat unappreciated, before cooking was "cool" and Pinterest recipes were all the rage. She faithfully set the stage for daily family contact around the dinner table. It wasn't until I began cooking and shopping and planning on my own, and then for my young family, that I began to realize the magnitude of what she had pulled off for decades.

In its simplicity, I had missed it. In my mom's lack of demand of attention for the service she provided, I failed to appreciate what all went into it. (But don't worry. She's getting the last laugh on this one, since I grew up and became responsible for getting dinners for my family of ten on the table. Which is a whole other study.)

I had a lot more revelations like this as I made my way through college, bought my first car, began work in radio and television, got married, started having babies, and bought our first home. (Air filters? That have to be replaced? Is that a thing?) Getting tax returns completed. Getting the inspection done on the car every year. It wasn't that my parents hadn't prepared me for many of these responsibilities—in fact, my brothers and I had chore charts to fill out each week. My dad was literally a rocket scientist and my mom an accountant. It turned out they were raising a passel of creatives, but they were determined we would be functional. They provided us with a good working knowledge of what we would be responsible for and how to get those things done, but there was so much more to the daily requirements of running a household and getting the bills paid and making the grocery store run and generally being a grown-up than I ever understood—until I was the one on the hook for getting those things done.

**When you were a child, what were some things you took for granted that just got done or were provided for you, things that were taken care of until you were the one who was responsible for them? Circle those items below, and add a few others that came as a big surprise when you hit the world of #adulting.**

**Laundry**

**Meal prep**

**Finances**

**Taxes**

**Household chores**

**Car maintenance (getting gas, changing the oil, etc.)**

**Making dental, medical appointments, etc.**

Others:

Even now, it is still amazing to me that the trash needs to go out every week and that my kids will, without fail, completely destroy the kitchen pantry within forty-eight hours of my attempt to turn it into a Pinterest-worthy scene of serene organization.

Life, and life with people, is so . . . daily. And it all requires maintenance. The kind of maintenance that shows up consistently, gets the job done without wasting time on drama, and then shows up again the next day.

**What are some things that you're still struggling to make part of your routine—things that you know need to be done but that still seem to evade you?**

*Balancing a check book*

When I look back on pictures from my childhood, now from the perspective of a woman who is holding down the fort, making sure the bills are paid on time, and seeing that the kids are in reasonably clean underwear, I'm attuned to the little details in those fading photographs of the past. I'm more aware than ever that, yes, my parents provided some truly photo album-worthy experiences of camping trips and holidays and road trips, but that it was in the faithful carrying out of those everyday, mundane duties, which seem almost invisible, that makes up the context and backdrop of my childhood. Had my parents not been so efficient and consistent in performing those seemingly mundane tasks, the road to some of the more complex elements of my childhood—getting my education, navigating the dangerous waters of girl-world social intrigue, and exploring my faith in our church community—would have been so much harder. That willingness to bridge the daily-ness of life to the bigger things my parents wanted me to be able to explore created that stable span of moving from childhood to adulthood over the choppy waters of my preteen and teen years.

There are those tasks out there, those roles that we sometimes play, that don't seem all that intriguing or historic or wildly within how we define our "purpose," but they are so, so important. I'm all about wanting people to find their passions and chase after those things, but then who is supposed to make sure the trash gets taken out on a regular basis?

**Where in your roles as a manager, mom, boss, teacher, or mentor do you find the most resistance? In what ways do you get the most pushback? In what areas do you experience the most frustration?**

*meal planning*
*filing papers*

**Would you say that you are a more task-oriented person or a more people-oriented person? How do you find that this influences your approach to the to-do lists in your life?**

*I'm a little of both! I like to ✓ off completed tasks. But a choice to play well wen on.*

## Not All Superheroes Are Super Famous

We tend to focus a lot on the big names in the Bible—the writers, the heroes, the villains. But have you ever thought about the unsung heroes of the early church? Those who helped house missionaries. Those brave souls who hosted church in their homes, who risked their businesses and their reputations in their communities to follow this Jesus and the movement He began. The money they gave, the time they spent, the risks they took.

We can take for granted that the letters of Paul even exist. We accept it as a matter of course that he wrote to various churches and that his words gave them direction for next steps and spiritual precepts as those young churches formed and thrived. But let's pause for just a minute.

This was the first century. There was no organized mail delivery system that we know of for the regular folk. No e-mail. No social media. You may be thinking, *Well, obviously*. But don't miss the incredible challenge here of attempting to unite a ragtag band of believers into some kind of force for good. Communication was difficult, writing materials were precious and expensive, and transportation was slow and dangerous. So how was the policy and marketing plan for what would become the early church communicated? How did leadership initiatives and HR handbooks (if you will) make their way into the hands of those early gatherings of believers?

**Look up and read the following verses:**

Ephesians 6:21 *Tychicus*
Colossians 4:7 *Tychicus*
2 Timothy 4:12 *Tychicus*
Titus 3:12 *Artemas or Tychicus*

**What name did you find in each of these passages?**

*Tychicus*

Tychicus (pronounced TIH-kih-kuhs[1]). He was Paul's communication director, the "telephone line" that ran across the various baby churches developing across Asia Minor. His name means "fortuitous," as in *serendipity*, or what we would call a "lucky dog" in our jargon. The first time his name shows up in Scripture is during Paul's third missionary journey, following the account of Paul's quick departure from Ephesus, after he managed to make some locals pretty mad (this seems to be a theme for our sweet Paul). We know from a passage in Acts 20:2-6 that Tychicus was with Paul and several other men as they journeyed from Greece to Macedonia. Tychicus traveled ahead with some of the men to Troas, and Paul joined them a few days later.

Paul had been to Troas before, so this would have been a return trip for him. Troas was a Greek city located on the coast of the Aegean Sea. For a Greek town, it was under considerable Roman influence; the aqueduct constructed for the city is still there today, along with the ruins of the old walls and towers, the gymnasium, and the baths. It was also an important seaport with a robust business of transporting passengers to many places across Europe.

Now, let's head out on a small tangent.

**Read Acts 20:7-12. This is the passage of Scripture immediately following the account of Tychicus and others being with Paul in Troas. What is the name of the young man mentioned in these verses?**

In verse 9 we're introduced to Eutychus, the young man who somewhat famously falls asleep during the apostle Paul's long sermon and tumbles from the window where he has been sitting to the ground three stories below. Those who scramble to reach him find him dead. But that is not Paul's diagnosis.

**Record below what Paul says in verse 10.**

Don't be alarmed     he's alive

**Now record what Paul does afterward in verse 11.**

goes upstairs Breaks bread + ate. after talking until daylight he left

**And let's gather one more little morsel from this passage. How much longer, according to verse 11, did Paul keep talking?**

all night long

Here's the thing that has kept Bible scholars chatting for years about this section of Scripture. The names Tychicus and Eutychus are essentially the same because both mean "fortuitous"—or again, "lucky dog," so to speak. So there are several scholars who argue that Tychicus could be considered a nickname for Eutychus and thus they could be one and the same person, the lucky dog who survived or was revived from a fall—not from grace but from lethal drowsiness.

Others dispute this, but whether it was Tychicus/Eutychus (as one and the same person) who experienced firsthand that three-story fall and woke up in the arms of Paul, or whether it was Tychicus who watched while a dozing Eutychus hit the pavement and Paul comforted those around him as the young man's eyes fluttered back open, Tychicus was there. He experienced, one way or another, Paul's marathon preaching session with a sidebar of midnight miracle.

**What do you think being part of that experience would do for Tychicus's loyalty and devotion to Paul?**

Well, if Tychicus's was in fact Eutychus he was totally grateful. Awe struck. He owed his life to Him.

You may have never noticed the name Tychicus before. And that doesn't make you a haphazard Bible reader. We tend to notice events over names when it comes to more thrilling events or more familiar characters. But taking notice of the name Tychicus and considering some interesting details we find in the Word help us begin to understand more of his story, his motivation, and his impact.

---

# 2

---

*I want to be a bridge that leads to You*
*So reach through me*

"The Bridge," Mark John Hall, Bernie Herms,
Seth David Mosly, Matthew Joseph West

## Connectors Needed

I've been serving on the staff of my home church for many years now as the women's ministry lead. I don't know how other churches handle that position, but for me it means that I speak a lot, create study content, and provide pastoral counsel. But it also means that I'm an event planner. We have multiple big events every year at our church, events that we hope will draw in members of the community who may be looking for a church or who may be ready to explore faith. We have concerts, musical productions, seminars, conferences, social gatherings, and more.

Now, as a mom of eight kids, I can pull off an event. I mean, even just surviving Christmas morning with a crew this size means that I must, somewhere, have some event planning skills. So I do okay at it. And I've managed to get many events off the ground and to the finish line each year within my ministerial work.

But let me tell you, it doesn't come naturally for me. For years I was a nervous wreck before every event of which I was in charge. I wasn't nervous about what my message would be at an event; that seemed to always flow, and I always was in the center of what I was supposed to be doing on that front. But heavens. What turned my cuticles into a shredded state and my heart rate into jackrabbit status were all the details and what I might forget in terms of water bottles and swag and ticket issues and catering and print materials and hotels for the musical guest and on and on and on.

Eventually, I was blessed to build a team who locked arms with me and came alongside to help with all those millions of details. It enabled me to focus on the bigger picture of what we were wanting to accomplish at these events, while also honoring and making sure the "smaller details" that make an event feel welcoming and organized and peaceful were all covered. But I was still managing a lot of the details and making the assignments to my team of volunteers, being on call right up until I walked onstage. I'm so thankful and amazed by all the things my team has been willing to do and by how they have been so patient with all the places I've dropped the ball and had to scramble. And I still need each and every one of them in order to do all that we are doing.

But now . . . now I have a Tychicus.

Let's call her Jennifer. She gets flustered by the spotlight, even a written one. She would try to tell you that she's no big deal, that what she does is simple. She would do her dead level best to minimize what she does, but don't you fall for it. Jennifer has now come alongside me as the person who has scooped up a big portion of all those crazy details. And she. Just. Handles. It. Completely. Faithfully. She gathers those contracts and remembers which speaker is allergic to mint. She remembers to make sure there is gluten-free catering for that musical artist. She

thinks through what kinds of needs our event attendees will have, and she is on top of it. She'll check in with me on a couple of questions, but otherwise she figures it out and gets it done. And because she does that, because she is such a phenomenal bridge in connecting the big vision of whatever event we are hosting to the actual elements that are critical and crucial to carrying out that vision, she makes those events mean so much more than just throwing a big party. She bridges all those details to creating experiences for people to connect with each other and with Christ. She's someone who lives out the role of Tychicus with such beauty.

Can I tell you something about how we sometimes view the Tychicus tribe, those who are doing the bridge work of connecting the dots? It worries me—it really does—that we have made much of those who do the "stage" work, those who speak and perform music and pitch the big vision and land the enormous account. Even in our faith communities, we can elevate certain giftings and their expression as somehow more "spiritual" or of greater import.

*Be devoted to one another in love. Honor one another above yourselves.*

*Romans 12:10*

But just a quick perusal of Scripture clearly shows that this was not the vision Jesus had for His church.

**Read Romans 12:10 in the margin. What are the two actions this passage tells us to do for one another?**

1. Be devoted to one another in love

2. honor one another above yourself

Let's look at that first action you wrote down: *be devoted*. In the original Greek used in the writing of that passage by Paul, the word *devoted* has such a beautiful meaning. It is the kind of love and tenderness of a parent to a child. It's not just holding someone in esteem or having a general appreciation of a person. It's not just a vague sense of loyalty. It's the kind of connection that speaks of a tenderness, a care that is given regardless of the ability of the other party to reciprocate. To be devoted really does carry in the original language the idea of family. This is why Paul says we are to be devoted *in love*. It's not just devoted out of a sense of obligation. It's not devoted out of trying to climb some kind of church hierarchy—to become head usher or whatever position you covet. It's devoted from a place of cherishing others as your siblings in Jesus. It's being committed to your church family, not just "shopping" for a Sunday experience that meets all your preferences. The original word for

devoted in this passage is *philostrogos*, and it's a tenderness, a cherishing in the family sense. We throw around the phrase "church family," but are we living like it? Are we treating one another with that kind of preference and patience and pledge? We often "like" our church friends. We often "enjoy" being around them. But to fulfill the vision Paul carried for the church is something so much more.

That next action you wrote down, *honor*, is also a word we toss around a lot today, often in our concern that we don't show honor well in our culture. Usually by *honor* we mean some general sense of holding someone in esteem for the office they hold or the position they have earned. But *honor* has much more depth than that in the original language. It also means "a valuing by which the price is fixed."[2] And for us as believers in Jesus, that means each individual we encounter had his or her "price" or "value" set on a revolutionary day on a rocky hill in first-century Jerusalem when Jesus, the Son of God, was executed. Everyone you meet and deal with and love and like and struggle with? Their value before God is that they are worth the life of His Son.

In talking about showing honor, Paul includes the words *above your-selves*, meaning we are to honor each other above ourselves. That's where things get tricky, isn't it? It's a little easier to academically agree to honor people when it doesn't include making it above our own honor of self.

I can say I have love and honor for others but can really get twisted up when that love and honor ask that I lay down something I have a strong opinion about. But when we only practice a form of Christianity that is convenient to our schedule and in perfect keeping with the goals we designed for ourselves in January and is more predicated on our "vision" for ourselves than on the vision for the health and totality of the faith body, we can find it difficult to be a bridge into people's hearts.

When we show a "preference" for others, above our own agendas and preferences, we lead the way to show what honor is supposed to look like. We set the standard for what devotion is supposed to be.

Let's face it, we live in a culture of Christian celebrity. I've met with a lot of women who tell me they desire to "do something for the Lord," but they want whatever that something is to have lots of cool bells and whistles and acclaim and spotlight. They often want me to help develop their platform and "following." Now, listen. The word of God is clear that there are going to be those people who have more public roles in the Kingdom. It's not wrong for people to follow that leading if it comes from the Lord. But when I look at the ministry of Tychicus, I see that he was willing to act as the bridge for Paul to those baby Christians who so badly needed guidance. And we deeply need people in our faith communities who can do just that. It's just as important, just as critical as some of the roles of which we tend to make such a big deal. Tychicus was able to connect the gap.

In our modern faith communities today, we can feature all kinds of great talent, powerful speakers, amazing musicians. But it takes a person, a real, available person, who cares, who shows personal honor, who is willing to elevate others, to create that deep and lasting connection between the celebrated platform and the pew.

**Are there aspirations you've held that are well intended but may be holding you back from acting as a bridge in the lives of those around you? If so, how could you adjust your perspective to chase that dream—writing that book, performing that song, or accomplishing that other goal—while also leaving room, availability, and flexibility to engage as a bridge for someone else?**

*By the grace given me I say to every one of you: Do not think of yourself more highly than you ought, but rather think of yourself with sober judgment, in accordance with the faith God has distributed to each of you.*

*Romans 12:3*

**Take a look at Romans 12:3 in the margin. Paul is pretty direct in this passage. How would you summarize what he says?**

I want to encourage you to get in the habit of looking at verses from the angle of different translations. You don't need to go buy a whole shelf of Bibles in multiple translations (although, to me it seems like a great thing to add to your book collection! #bibliophile). You can go to any online Bible website and find all kinds of options for viewing Scripture through a variety of translations. As we look at the Romans 12:3 verse, I want you to see it from The Passion Translation (designated as TPT). The Passion Translation, like other translations, is based on the ancient Hebrew, Greek, and Aramaic texts, and it seeks to use our modern language to more fully reveal the heart and dynamic of Scripture. This is how The Passion Translation renders Romans 12:3:

*God has given me grace to speak a warning about pride. I would ask each of you to be emptied of self-promotion and not create a false image of your importance. Instead, honestly assess your worth by using your God-given faith as the standard of measurement, and then you will see your true value with an appropriate self-esteem.*

Wow. Those are some tough words there, Paul. We live in an era in which self-promotion, imaging, branding, and selfies are all the rage. I'm guilty, and you may be too. I've watched Christians—*Christians, people*—practically get into shoving matches trying to get their photo taken with someone they consider a Christian celebrity! What are we doing?

**Look up 1 Corinthians 1:10-17. What does Paul have to say about Christians behaving badly in this way?**

We are to follow Christ alone,

When we evaluate someone's "worth" in our faith circles based on how "popular" they are or how public their ministry is, we are missing the ability to see, honor, and appreciate those opportunities and people who can be the bridge between a great Christian concert or event and the real-life application of living out its message.

Let's take a heart check: who are some people you've elevated perhaps a bit too much in your faith walk? Is it your pastor? That favorite author or artist you love? That motivational speaker? Hear me well, we should honor those who lead us. It's a gift to find a teacher you resonate with. But if we are not careful, we can end up following a man or a woman over our Messiah. Do you find yourself possibly quoting that person or those persons more than you do Scripture? Do you find that the "truth" they present means more to you than the more challenging teachings of Scripture? Listen, me too. I struggle with the same things. So join me here.

**Let's take that heart check and pray it out. Let's confess before God if we have over-elevated others and reset our eyes on Him. Write out your confessional prayer below:**

People who motivate and inspire us are great. But we serve a Messiah who is far greater.

---

# 3

---

*Although you were once distant and far away from God, now you have been brought delightfully close to him through the sacred blood of Jesus—you have actually been united to Christ!*

Ephesians 2:13 TPT

## The Power of a Bridge

My husband, Michael, has had some pretty bland office views in his career. And he's had some pretty spectacular ones as well. His current office overlooks one of the most incredible views in the Austin, Texas, skyline. His office is situated on a cliff above Lake Austin. When he looks to the southeast, his line of sight can follow the lake all the way to an incredible view of downtown, nestled amongst the rolling limestone and cedar-fringed hills of the Texas Hill Country.

I like to think it makes up for the years when his view was the inside of a cubicle in an office that seemed to always be in some sort of remodel and electrical system crisis, with ceiling tiles missing and wires hanging down in questionable states of safety.

Now, if you're familiar with Austin or its reputation, then you've probably heard of our traffic. All those rumors would be true and then some. Just last night it took Michael almost two hours to make it the thirteen miles between his office and our home, a complicated recipe of rush hour and rain and multiple fender benders chewing through the commute clock and bringing things to a freeway standstill. So, yes, Michael spends a lot of time staring at the bumper in front of him.

But part of his commute is over a bridge that has become iconic in Austin. The Pennybacker Bridge spans Lake Austin and was opened in 1982. More than 600 million pounds of steel were used in its construction, and it cost ten million dollars to construct. It soars one hundred feet above the water below, and no part of the structure touches the lake. Its beautiful design has won an award and has become a must-see destination for those taking in the Austin sights and sounds.[3] But why Pennybacker? Where did that unusual name come from?

The bridge is not named after the designer or the builder. It's not named after a major financial contributor. It's named in honor of Percy Pennybacker. Percy Pennybacker was born in Palestine, Texas, and received his degree in civil engineering from the University of Texas at Austin. He developed a new technique for the welding of structures; in particular, bridges. A World War I veteran who served in the Army Air Service, he spent time in Kansas and Texas helping construct bridges, and his advancements in techniques for welding earned him accolades and awards. His unique contributions to welding and his advancement of using those innovations as an alternative to rivets have reportedly saved millions of dollars in the construction of bridges in the state. So, this beautiful bridge was named in his honor.

And there's another interesting note to his life. Percy Pennybacker had Type 1 diabetes, also known as juvenile diabetes. His father also had it and died of complications of the disease. When Percy was still early in his career as a civil engineer, his condition landed him in the hospital for almost a year. In an attempt to treat his diabetes, Percy Pennybacker became one of the first patients ever in history to receive insulin as a treatment.[4] So the next time you visit Austin or see a photograph of the bridge and take a little day hike on the limestone cliffs adjacent to the bridge, you'll know a little bit more about the guy behind the name of this iconic bridge. Percy Pennybacker. A footnote on the Austin, Texas, skyline.

Without that bridge, large sections of our city would not be accessible to one another. Without that bridge, Michael's commute wouldn't just be long: It would be almost impossible unless it also involved a ferryboat and then some kind of crane to lift him from the cliff that abuts the lake. Yet, even as important as that bridge is in our community, even as many cars as it creates a safe passage for each day, I'd lived here many years before I ever bothered to find out why it was called the Pennybacker Bridge.

We don't celebrate enough those who act as the bridge, those who keep their heads down as they keep things running and manage the details and think through what welds it all together. The behind-the-scenes heroes. Those who shy away from accolades but plan all the details to celebrate the giving of said accolades.

In my office is a small leather-bound book. It's my paternal grandfather's Bible. He was a quiet, reserved man, the perfect match to my paternal grandmother's more emotive personality. He lived a simple life, farming in central Mississippi when the crops were good, and then working in the shipyards on the Mississippi coast when the crops went bad. We would spend a few days each summer with him and my grandmother when we were kids—that part of the world seeming exotic compared to our Southern California high-desert home. He died when I was ten, and so the memories of the time I had with him are few. But I love having his little Bible, the one he carried with him each Sunday.

And catch this: his name was Allen Bridges Lyles. Yep. Bridges. It was his paternal grandmother's maiden name—my great-great-grandmother on that side, Virginia "Jennie" Bridges Lyles. I wish I knew more about her life, about her marriage to my great-great-grandfather James Madison Lyles. There are very few details in the family records on her life. But what I do know is that she was significant enough to her son that he wanted his own son to carry her name, hence my grandfather's moniker of Allen Bridges Lyles.

**Who has been a bridge in your life, connecting you to a fuller walk with the Lord?**

**What kind of divine connections have you experienced in your life—those friendships, situations, or experiences that led to a powerful new chapter in your life?**

**Has there been a time the Lord has used you in a unique way to connect others to one another or to God? If so, write about it briefly.**

*I learned that a long walk and calm conversation are an incredible combination if you want to build a bridge.*

—Seth Godin[5]

## You Span Somebody's Today and Tomorrow

I was in my late twenties with two little girls, a little-bitty mortgage that went with a little-bitty house, and a husband who was working hard and gone a lot. We had started going to a church a bit closer to that little-bitty house, and it was at that church that I met a woman who would become a bridge for me. Her name was Lanna. Her youngest child was about the age of my oldest child, so she had navigated the parenting waters a few years longer than I had. She was fun and outgoing. And she was very passionate about Bible study. She invited me to the Bible study they held weekly at this church, where I met several other women I enjoyed and connected with.

The Bible study itself was beyond anything I had experienced before. I'd been raised in a Christian home, in a church that considered itself very biblically based. I mean, I could have smoked anybody in a Bible trivia round from all that I received in my upbringing. The Christian university I graduated from required hours of credit in Bible, regardless of your degree plan. But this new Bible study, with these new friends, it was so deep. It was an inductive study called Precept, developed by Kay Arthur.[6] We learned how to dive into the original language. We learned how to better understand context, repeated phrases, connections to other verses in the Bible. We worked through intense homework. After two or three years of attending this study, I decided to become certified in this method of study and attended classes and walked through a certification process.

Now, understand, Lanna didn't write these studies. She didn't check my homework, force me to come to the gathering, or reinforce every lesson with commentary and cajoling. Nope. She was the bridge, the scaffold that connected me to an experience that I can absolutely point back to as foundational in all that would follow, from ending up in vocational ministry to writing, podcasting, and speaking. Because Lanna was willing to be a bridge, it bridged me to the calling and purpose God had for my life. She wasn't trying to tie me to her, to her mission, or to her particular small group. She was simply willing to be a conduit, without agenda, that led me to a fuller understanding of following God and falling more deeply in love with His Word.

God has put people in your life who need you as a bridge. They've come to a ridgeline in their lives. They may not even realize what they are looking for or know what God has on the horizon for them. It's not my job or yours to jump in and receive all revelation for this person and create some layered accountability for her or him. And most people don't even need that. What they do need is someone who is simply willing to connect them to God. Someone who is willing to invite them to the small group. Someone who is willing to listen to them when you chance to meet in the grocery store aisle. Someone who is willing to share a smile, extend a hand, be present with them. It's a responsibility placed on each of us, whatever our gifts and talents, whatever our calling.

**Read John 13:1-17. It's such a familiar passage to many of us, but let's read it with fresh eyes. What stands out to you? Write your thoughts below.**

I keep coming back to the last part of verse 1, which suggests that what Jesus does for the disciples in the verses that follow is part of showing them the full extent of His love.

**Understanding that we are to serve one another, how do we make sure we are not being sidelined by busywork or activated by a debilitating need within us to people please? How do we make sure we are doing God's work and not just trying to keep the peace?**

**Write Leviticus 25:17 below.**

*Martha was distracted by all the preparations that had to be made. She came to him and asked, "Lord, don't you care that my sister has left me to do the work by myself? Tell her to help me!"*

*Luke 10:40*

**Now read Luke 10:40 in the margin. How is Martha described in this verse?**

Perhaps an important evaluation tool we need when looking at opportunities to serve is to determine if we're being drawn closer to the Lord or if we're getting distracted by the details. And for leaders, it's critical that we observe if we are allowing those with serving, hospitality, and administration gifts to become overcommitted and overstressed. I love Jesus's clarification for all our programs and details and scurrying: one thing is needed. One. And that is to experience Him.

**How do we keep Jesus as our focus when serving? How do we avoid becoming distracted like Martha? How do we avoid taking advantage of others who have servant hearts?**

There's a beautiful part of the structure of a song called the musical bridge, a place in the music that builds and connects the stanzas and the choruses for us. The legendary group The Beatles has been well celebrated for its musical bridges in its iconic songs. A great musical bridge makes the power of a song even more heightened, and it creates a connection for the listener between all the elements of the song.

Let us take on the role of being a bridge in the symphony of this life, in this new song of God. It's as simple as being a kind friend, a listening ear, a thoughtful neighbor. In so doing, without needing to have all the right words and strategies, we become a connection for people to a loving God. We become part of this tribe of Tychicus—those willing to connect, support, love, dot the i's and cross the t's. The bridges.

## Tychicus
### The Bridge

*We can become a connection for people to a loving God.*

### Welcome/Prayer/Icebreaker (5-10 minutes)

Welcome to Session 1! Over the next four weeks, we're going to look at four minor characters in the Bible who teach us some major lessons. Today we're exploring what Tychicus has to teach us about being a "bridge"—one who connects, supports, serves, and loves others. Open with prayer. Then go around the circle and tell of someone who is a valuable, "behind-the-scenes" kind of person in your life.

### Video (about 20 minutes)

Play the "Getting Started: A Devotional Reflection" video (optional), taking a couple of minutes to focus your hearts and minds on God's Word. Then play the video segment for Session 1, filling in the main idea as you watch and making notes about anything that resonates with you or that you want to be sure to remember.

---

## —Video Notes—

**Scripture**: Colossians 4:7-8

**Main Idea**: Not all of us have to be in the driver's seat, but all of us can be a

_____.

**Other Insights**:

---

## Group Discussion (20-25 minutes for a 60-minute session; 30-35 minutes for a 90-minute session)

### Video Discussion

- How can you be a bridge by helping connect the message of Jesus to those who desperately need to hear it? In what ways has the Lord been leading you to engage with others and walk with them?

### Workbook Discussion

- Take turns reading aloud Ephesians 6:21; Colossians 4:7; 2 Timothy 4:12; and Titus 4:12. What do we know about Tychicus?
- Read aloud Romans 12:3 and 10. What do we learn from these verses about serving with humility?
- Do you think there is a potential danger in the church for those with more public gifts to be "elevated" or celebrated more often? Do you find yourself more drawn to those who are more public in the church experience? Why or why not?
- How do we make sure that the quieter gifts, the more hidden contributions, are also appreciated?
- What kind of divine connections have you experienced in your life—those friendships, situations, or experiences that led to a powerful new chapter in your life? (page 25)
- Read aloud John 13:1-17. What can we learn from Jesus's example about how to serve others?
- Are you willing to do the small things, the little jobs, the unnoticed chores that seem little but have such reach? Or do you fight the idea of spending your time on that?
- How do we keep Jesus as our focus when serving? How do we avoid becoming distracted like Martha? (page 28)
- Maybe you've seen those with more public gifts and callings take advantage of those with servant hearts in supportive, bridge roles. How can we avoid the pitfall of expecting things to just get done regardless of time constraints and other challenges?

## One to One (10-15 minutes – 90 minute session only)

Divide into groups of 2-3 and discuss the following:

- Who has been a bridge in your life, connecting you to a fuller walk with the Lord? (page 25)
- How has the Lord used you in a unique way to connect others? (page 25)

## Closing Prayer (5 minutes)

Close the session by sharing personal prayer requests and praying together. In addition to praying out loud for one another, ask God to help you follow Jesus's example to serve others in humility and love, becoming bridges that connect people to our loving God.

# Week 2

## Joanna

### The Messenger

## 1

*"God has given us two hands—one to receive with and the other to give with. We are not cisterns made for hoarding; we are channels made for sharing."*

Billy Graham, *The Quotable Billy Graham* (1966)

### "They"

There are a lot of things in this crazy world of ours that I think somebody should do something about.

For example, how bizarre is it that we live in a world that has learned to automate so many things, and yet I find that I continue to have to practice, week in and week out, one of the most inefficient cycles I know of in modern life: grocery shopping. I drive to the grocery store (or, in my case, the big warehouse kind of places that have groceries and other items in bulk sizes—because, eight kids). Grab a cart. Find and select an item from the shelf. Put it in said cart. Repeat sixty-four more times with various items. Then go the checkout lane and take all those items out of the cart. Have a clerk handle and scan every item you've already handled. Then put all those items back in that same cart. Push that cart out to your fifteen-passenger van. (Don't be jealous! We can't all drive such a high-performance machine). Unload that cart yet one more time into your vehicle, just so you can drive home and undo the process and unload each item yet again.

*Sisters.* Can we just agree there are some unnecessary steps in all of this? Like, if Facebook can keep track of my every move, surely there should be a way that I can enter that store, load that cart one time, and be on my merry way. I know that Amazon is working on improving this whole strange practice, and I salute Sam's Club for its new "Scan and Go" app, but still. Somebody should have done something long ago about this archaic practice, am I right?

*Somebody.* Surely, those people out there, the big retailers and the computer people and those techy kinds of people, *they* should have figured this out by now, right? So that I don't have to be inconvenienced by all the extra cart loading and unloading.

Ah, *They.* The magical population out there made up of people and organizations that we think should be making progress or whose opinions we fear or whose rules we follow because *They say*:

> Don't wear white after Labor Day.
> Don't drink milk after a tummy bug.
> Starve a fever, feed a cold . . . or is it starve a cold, feed
>     a fever? (I never can remember that one correctly.
>     #momfail)
> If you pluck that gray hair, you'll get twice as many more.
> If you crack your knuckles, you'll get arthritis.
> Don't you swallow that gum! It will take you seven years
>     to digest it!

**What are some "rules" you remember being taught, things having to do with what to wear and when, dietary rules, edicts about kid-raising, church etiquette, and others?**

*- don't eat for 8⁶ hrs after vomiting.*
*- don't wear white after labor day.*
*- Carrots are good for your eyes*
*- liver - pure protein*

**Did you ever wonder where these came from? Which ones did you think made sense? Which ones confused you?**

*Some made sense. Some I just followed because my parents told me. Some because it was fashion sense.*

**Have you ever looked into where some of these *They* rules came from? Were the rules based on truth and wisdom or**

**do they seem to have come from someone's preferences or culture?**

*Some made sense to me.
Some I didn't care about.*

**Read 1 Timothy 4:7 in the margin and record below what Paul seems to call some of those rules and expectations and stories of *They*.**

*godless myths – wives tales*

> *Have nothing to do with godless myths and old wives' tales; rather, train yourself to be godly.*
>
> *1 Timothy 4:7*

The Greek root word for "old wives' tales" is *mythos*, and it means what you would expect it to—those stories and sayings that are based in myths instead of truth. The most literal translation reads "fables only fit of old women." Um, ouch, Paul. Seems a little harsh. But it can also be translated *anile*, which is a word we get from the Latin that is a metaphor, meaning in this case the idea of someone who is doddering around like a little old lady, mumbling to herself. So I'm thinking what Paul means here is that we don't want to take as truth those sayings and stories of culture that are for someone who no longer wants to learn truth, who prefers to just wander around repeating the same things to ourselves over and over. (Today that would include fake news and Snopes-disproved urban legends.)

**What are some things you accepted in the past as real simply because you heard them so many times, only to later discover they had no basis in research or truth? How did following some of those directives impact certain events in your life—from how you organized your house or what color you wore to that friend's wedding to how you interacted with others?**

One of the bigger throwdowns I had with my mom as we were planning my wedding was over the wording and order of the wedding invitation. My fiancé and I wanted a more casual wording on the invitation, and my mom was horrified. She was genuinely shaken. "What will people think?" was the hallmark question of those discussions. For her, there was a presiding *They* that dictated the correct verbiage and order of a wedding invitation, and that *They* must be obeyed in order to avoid . . . well, I'm still not really clear on what the dire consequences would have been if Michael and I had insisted on the original wording we wanted; but it certainly seemed that it would be dire. We laugh about it now, and I'd like to think that I've not succumbed to the tyranny of the *They* rules in other decisions, but that wouldn't be true. We too often blindly accept these rules from that mysterious tribe called *They*.

*They* have all kinds of opinions and thoughts about how to raise kids and treat laundry and how often your oil should be changed. *They* have directives about nutrition, holidays, and travel. *They* are quite verbose. It goes a little something like this: "Well, you know what *They* say . . ."

But *They* also have a lot of pressure on them. It's not just social niceties and fashion dictums that rest on their shoulders. *They* should fix the government, figure out our health care crisis, and resolve issues in education. *They* should do something. *They* should fix it.

You can also find *They* in church life. *They* should start a ministry to address that need. *They* should do something about the music volume. *They* should do something about that single mom who is struggling.

*They*.

As much as I've held *They* responsible for several things in the political, technological, and humanitarian realms, I've had a bit of a shock in recent years. I've been in vocational ministry for over a decade now, meaning that I make part of my living by serving on a church staff as the leader of women's ministry. And here's the shock: there are people who think I'm *They*. What?! I'm now the frustrating, vague-rule-making, unactionable *They* who should know better and do better and fix things? Me? I've never been a fan of that mysterious tribe of *They*. So how did I become one?

## Making Assignments for *They*

Best I can tell, the process goes like this. Let's say someone discovers there is a group of single moms who need help with maintenance on their homes. This person will get fired up, appropriately, about the plight of these moms who are working so hard to provide for their families and keep their kids in church and run all the things for their homes. Or perhaps someone finds that a woman who would like to come to Bible study can't afford the materials. Or maybe it's that the school down the road is struggling to provide classroom resources to students. So I get an email. Or sometimes someone will schedule a meeting with me to make me aware of a situation they have learned about, a challenge in the community that they are passionate about. That passion to help is fantastic; that instinct to let people know about the needs they've discovered is pure.

But here's where it takes a weird turn. "*You* should do something about it," this person will tell me in an e-mail or meeting, their finger pointing. "*The church* should take care of this. It's shameful *you're* letting this go unaddressed." And then the conversation will expand, with assertions that *They*, meaning the church staff, should be doing something to resolve the needs in the community, the places of lack.

Listen, I'm not reverse finger pointing here. I myself have shot off some emails and had meetings like that, directing the conversation to that *They* out there that I thought should take action. And I'm not here to shame anyone who may have ever sent one of those emails or left a voice mail with similar content.

But I have come to believe this: when it comes to the church, I am *They*.

And so are you.

*They* are us. We are *They*.

There is no church without us. There is no Bride without us filling her frame, bringing movement and life to her purpose. I love a beautiful church building as much as you. I adore a well-designed church program that creates momentum and clarity. I appreciate a church that has a well-defined organizational chart with fully developed definitions of various church staff positions and responsibilities. I delight in church events that inspire and activate.

But none of that *is* the church.

*We* are the church. All of us. Whatever our gifts may be—whether or not we are on staff, are ordained, or ever went to Bible college or seminary. There's no secret council behind the curtain pulling the levers. No bureaucracy to spoon-feed us and keep us docile.

Us. We are it. We are the messengers of Christ. We are the church. *Church* is a verb and we are that verb, that action that carries the message of Christ. May we be it well.

Holding the view that the staff and the pastors are responsible for all the care and evangelism of the community is misguided. When we operate from this place in our philosophy of church, it can remove the responsibility each of us has to be a messenger of Christ. It can make us passive. It can allow us to procrastinate an assignment God has given us as we look for an "expert" or a "specialist" to take action.

That's what I so appreciate about our Footnote this week, a woman named Joanna. She's only mentioned by name twice in the Gospel of Luke. I don't know exactly why Luke decided to record her name while Matthew, Mark, and John did not. As we talk about in this session's video, it may have been to honor her for the details and information she was able to share with Luke based on her close proximity to the court of Herod Antipas, the Jewish ruler of the time. Part of it may be found in the fact that Luke, as a physician and a gatherer of details and evidence, may have felt it was important to be clear about the wide range of people Jesus drew to Himself in the scope of His ministry here on earth.

Joanna was one of the people who didn't "need" to involve herself in some rogue upstart of a Jewish cult. She had connections. She had resources. She had position. Despite all of that, she still knew she needed Jesus.

**Read Luke 8:1-3 and jot down any details that stand out to you from this passage.**

Part of what we see in this passage is a description of Joanna as the wife of Chuza, the "manager" or "steward" of Herod's household, depending on the Bible translation you prefer to read. That word, *manager*, could seem to have a lot of various meanings to us, but in the original Greek it is the term *epitropos*, which carries a lot of weight.

Historians tell us that this position was one that meant a person oversaw the estate of the noble, overseeing all the staff, purchases, and needs of the business, buildings, and lands of the estate. Now, let's be clear: Herod was living large, my friends. His father, Herod the Great, had built a massive palace complex in Jerusalem and was the one to whom the wise men initially came seeking the Child they found in the message of the star. Herod the Great ultimately killed off all the Hebrew baby boys up to the age of two in an effort to wipe out that Child and the threat to the throne that Herod believed He represented. Charming guy. So his son, Herod Antipas, the one whom Chuza was serving, had a vast palace complex. A historian who lived at this time, Josephus, said in his writing that the palace had pools and gardens and three large towers that stood like sentinels over all the comings and goings there. The remains of this palace can be visited today. It boasted a plumbing and sewage system. It wasn't just a palace; it was also a fortress, with military innovation built into the structure. There are also those who believe that this palace may have been the site of the trial of Jesus.[1]

The two huge wings of the palace held many rooms and could accommodate guests into the hundreds. The irrigation systems required to maintain the many pools and water features were complex. To have overseen the management of such a facility would have been a massive job, with a huge staff of people required to maintain, clean, repair, serve, decorate, and garden. But this was not the only palace that Herod Antipas could frequent, as there were other palaces available to him throughout the region. Which means that Chuza may well have overseen not only the palace complex at Jerusalem but also several other estates on Herod's behalf.[2]

So that's the kind of "manager" we're talking about in Chuza, not someone overseeing a nice little country house with a couple of stables and guest cottages out back. We're talking about places like the Opryland Hotel in Nashville and the Gaylord Texan Resort in Dallas. And then some. Chuza had some serious career going on. And Joanna was married to him.

**What kinds of things do you think Joanna could have been privy to because of her marriage to Chuza? What details do you think she might have known about when it came to Herod Antipas?**

Given Chuza's position and perhaps Joanna's own noble standing in possibly coming from a notable family line, she, according to Luke, was able to help in funding the ministry of Jesus.

**Read Matthew 14:1-12. The Herod you are reading about there is Herod Antipas, the Herod whom Chuza serves. What do you learn about Herod from this passage? List everything you notice.**

What stands out to me is Herod Antipas's fascination with this Jesus he has been told about. He knows about some of the miracles that Jesus is performing. And yet he still chooses to execute John, the cousin of Jesus.

Herod Antipas was a complicated guy. He was not his father's first choice for taking leadership of the country. Initially, Herod the Great had it all set up that at his death, the kingdom would be split into three portions, with the three oldest sons—who were half brothers—each receiving territories. Herod Antipas was supposed to be left out in the cold on this deal as the youngest son. But his brother Herod Antipater, who was the oldest, developed a nasty habit of trying to poison their father, and things didn't end well for him. This meant that Herod Antipas ended up being granted one of those portions of the kingdom after his brother's fall and ultimately took over more of the territory. He was married twice, the second time to a niece and former wife of his brother. He was always juggling on a high wire in the wind, with the Roman occupiers looking over his shoulder at every decision or complication in the region. He wanted to prove himself as a leader, and he had to be cautious to not go too far and anger the Roman prefect of the region, Pilate. He had John the Baptist put to death at the request of one of his wives' daughters (Matthew 14:6-12). He demanded a miracle out of Jesus and laughed at Him when Jesus remained silent to Herod's questions and interrogation (Luke 23:8-12).[3]

Herod was unpredictable, opportunistic, and dangerous. And it was Joanna's husband who was by position embroiled in the whole mess.

**What kind of risk do you think Joanna was taking by following this Jesus who both fascinated and confounded Herod?**

So, to be clear, Joanna was someone who most likely was well versed in all of the crazy that was the Herod household. Surely she knew of his moods and his violence. And she still continued to follow the Jesus who presented such a problem for her husband's boss. She challenges me. She really does. With her family's livelihood and her husband's reputation on the line, not to mention her own safety, she followed Jesus. Can I say I would do the same in the face of such obstacles? Would you? Let it sit on your heart a bit as I'm letting it sit on mine.

---

# 2

---

*You never know how much you really believe anything until its truth or falsehood becomes a matter of life and death to you.*

C. S. Lewis, A *Grief Observed* (1963)

## Several Accounts, One Message

It's perhaps the most dramatic scene in the Bible, at least to my heart and mind: the moment when a group of women discovers that Jesus, the man of controversial ministry and mournful crucifixion, has somehow escaped the tomb meant to hold back His momentum.

**Let's read the account in Luke 24 about the events following the Crucifixion and burial of Jesus. Read verses 1 through 12, and make note below of things that stand out to you about this scene.**

There are accounts of the women going to the tomb in each Gospel. Some people have tried to argue that some of the details in these accounts contradict each other. Let's dig in together and see what we think.

**Complete the following chart:**

| Look up the passages below: | Who are the women in this passage? | What is the condition of the tomb? | To whom do the women speak? What instructions are they given? |
|---|---|---|---|
| Matthew 28:1-8 | | | |
| Mark 16:1–10 | | | |
| Luke 24:1-12 | | | |
| John 20:1-2 | | | |

One thing we sometimes get snarled in is the assumption that each Gospel writer should have made note of every single detail each other Gospel writer did. But we fail to remember that each of the Gospels allows us to have an enhanced angle of perception—one of the reasons I believe God wanted us to have four of them. Sometimes we tend to call something contradictory that actually is not. Matthew focuses primarily on two of the Marys. Mark lists an additional Mary and adds Salome. Luke throws in Joanna and Susanna. And John primarily focuses on Mary Magdalene at the tomb. Let's remember, simply because all of the same names aren't mentioned in each account doesn't mean they all weren't there. Luke, ever our detail guy, is careful to state in Luke 24:10 not just the names of Mary Magdalene, Joanna, and Mary the mother of James but also "and the others with them." So clearly there were several women who were part of this experience of discovering a tomb with the stone rolled away.

**What might be a possible reason the different Gospel writers chose to focus on the specific women they did? You might refer**

back to the chart. (There is no right or wrong answer here. This is just a question to get us thinking about the fact that each Gospel writer had a specific audience and purpose for his writing.)

In each of the accounts, what is the position of the stone that was to be blocking the entrance to the tomb?

Look back at Matthew 27:57-65. What were the instructions given by Pilate to the Pharisees regarding their concerns about the security of the tomb?

Now read Matthew 28:11-15. What became the Pharisees' backup plan?

In all of these Gospel accounts, the women receive an assignment beyond their original mission of bringing spices for the body of Jesus. What is it?

For a bonus round, look again at the passage in Mark 16. It has given people trouble because, at first glance, verse 8 seems to suggest the women didn't do what they had been assigned in verse 7, which was to tell Peter and the others about the resurrection of Jesus. But keep reading.

**What do you find that the women did in verse 10?**

When we look at the Mark passage in fuller context, we discover that verse 8 doesn't mean the women never said anything to anyone. We find that Mary specifically told who she was supposed to, and the women didn't tell others they encountered as they left the tomb because those were people they had not been told to tell.

**What do these verses say to you about the importance of making sure we read difficult Bible passages fully—and for detail?**

The women have been given the awesome responsibility of reporting what they have seen to the disciples. To really understand the significance of this, we have to refresh our context. Women in this culture would have likely been the last people entrusted with "breaking news." Something of this magnitude, in the mores of the times, would have been given to a high-ranking religious figure, a priest. In this situation, you would expect that Peter or John would have been the first to stumble upon the open tomb. Instead, it's a group of women. And Luke is clear that the disciples do not believe the women at first.

**Why do you think it was women to whom the incredible revelation that Jesus had risen from the dead was first given?**

I love that Joanna didn't look around for someone else to go tell the apostles what she had experienced. She didn't look for some kind of council or action group or hotline to go convey this message. She didn't allow herself to be paralyzed by her position as a woman in a male-dominated culture. She didn't seek the "experts." Instead, she saw the empty grave and heard from the angels about the risen Jesus. She went with Mary Magdalene, Mary the mother of James, and the other women who were with them and told the apostles what they had experienced.

Mission accomplished.

The women didn't suggest that the apostles should do something about it, that there should be a committee to investigate what they had seen, that they should get the news out through first-century "social media" that Jesus was no longer in the grave.

Joanna and the other women simply finished what had been given to them to do. And note, the apostles didn't believe them. Nope.

**Do you sometimes find that you would be willing to be a messenger of the good news of Jesus but then reconsider, worried that people won't believe you?**

**How does it impact you to realize that the apostles didn't believe the women?**

**Did the fact that the apostles didn't believe the women change the responsibility they had been given to make sure the apostles knew?**

**What does this say to you about your responsibility to act as a messenger without getting caught up in whether or not the message you share is accepted or rejected?**

Sometimes I resist being the messenger because I have too much of my own "identity" tied up in the message of the message, if you will. How will people think of me if I talk to them about the Lord? What if I can't convince them? What if they see me differently after I deliver this information? It's a good thing to wrestle, the difference between being the messenger and the bigger message we are responsible to carry.

---

# 3

---

*God Almighty declares the word of the gospel with power, and the warring women of Zion deliver its message.*

Psalm 68:11 TPT

## Somebody Should Do Something . . . And That Somebody Might Be You

It was 2001. I was pregnant with my fifth child and was quickly getting to that surreal size that you hit when you've carried a whole bunch of babies and you have no abdominal muscles left. (And this one would prove to be my biggest baby.) The pregnancy was going well, with its attendant fatigue and bulkiness, particularly while I was caring for my other four littles. I was in a season of full-on homeschooling with those four kiddos of mine, and while I had some concerns about how that was going, particularly because one of the kids seemed to be having issues with her speech, I was keeping an eye on things. But I was primarily concerned about my husband's work life. Michael had hit a major challenge at work, with a situation in which a peer was revoking what was contractually due him, and we were in the midst of making a huge change to a new firm. We were experiencing all the frustration and fear that go with discovering someone you trusted has been unethical, with the attendant concerns of the unknown of a new work environment. That was what was most immediate on my worry radar at the time, so when I made a routine appointment with an audiologist to evaluate my fourth child, Maesyn—the one who seemed a little speech delayed—I didn't even think to ask Michael to come along, given all the drama he was navigating. This was going to be a routine kind of doctor visit, just a little check-in to reassure me that all was well, that Maesyn was just taking her time with language.

Um, that was not the way that appointment turned out. At all. That little "routine" audiological booth test revealed that Maesyn had significant hearing loss, that she would need to be fitted for hearing aids, that we would need to make all kinds of therapy and educational and lifestyle decisions. One little twenty-minute booth test changed every minute that would follow.

Over the coming weeks, there was obviously a whole lot that had to be processed. There was a huge learning curve, as no one in our family or among our friends had dealt with pediatric hearing loss. There was guilt. Did I not take enough prenatal vitamins when I was pregnant with her? Should I have nursed her longer? On and on . . . the enemy loves to do a number on us when we're raw and vulnerable, doesn't he? There was worry about what this would mean for her future. But there were also some maddening discoveries.

As it turns out, due to a loophole in ERISA law (the Employee Retirement Income Security Act of 1974), many health insurance companies at that time were able to avoid paying for hearing aids for children if they were not considered "medically necessary." Yep. And here's where it gets really fun. The kinds of hearing aids that are needed for pediatric hearing loss cost thousands of dollars. Thousands and thousands, my friends. The kind of thousands that would take you on that dream anniversary trip to Paris one of these days. As a young family with four little kids and another one on the way, we were stunned emotionally and financially by this development.

I fought with insurance specialists. I called any and every one I could think of. I pleaded with the audiologist's office to intercede. I phoned attorneys, and I went back to the insurance company and demanded to speak with the manager of the insurance specialists—and then the manager of the manager. I took notebooks full of notes and educated myself on ERISA law and wrung my hands and cried and prayed and cried some more.

"Somebody should do something," I wrote in the margins of all those notes and phone numbers and email addresses. "Somebody should do something."

The *They* in charge of hearing aid coverage for toddlers was making me mama-kind-of-mad, which I'm sure you know is one of the purest kinds of rage in the universe.

But after all the kicking and screaming and financial scrambling, at the end of the day I needed to focus on Maesyn and her needs. Somebody should do something, but I sure didn't think it was me. I had to focus on my little girl and what I could do to equip her.

Fast-forward nine years.

That "somebody" became me. And it became Maesyn. In 2010, we were honored to start a nonprofit called 2dance2dream that offers dance for individuals who are differently abled.[4] It's a way we've been able to make a financial difference for families who are having to cover the cost of co-pays and expensive therapies and medical devices for their children with special needs. It doesn't fix the questionable practices of insurance companies regarding needed medical technology for kids, but it does give families a program for their kids to experience dance and performance arts through the generosity of sponsors and donors.

Six years later, Maesyn and I returned to her birth state in 2016 for her to speak in front of state representatives and senators and policy makers to assert the right and need for children identified with hearing loss to have access to hearing technology through grants and financial assistance. Oklahoma, through a nonprofit called Hearts for Hearing, is one of the few states in the nation that helps provide hearing aids for all newly identified children in the state.[5] There are surely many more miles to go on this, and we still need insurance reform, education for lawmakers, and so much more. But things, they are a-changing.

Sisters, I would never ever have thought that I could have made a hill of beans' worth of difference back when I sat in that audio booth with Maesyn and realized that she couldn't hear the tones being blasted from the speakers behind us. I never would have thought that the day would come when Maesyn would so beautifully advocate for the next generation of kids being identified with hearing loss. I wanted somebody to do something. I wanted somebody to do something right in the middle of our pain. I wanted somebody to do something, but I wanted it to be the *They* who live in that fog of blame and hurt and confusion and fear.

Instead, I realize now that I'd been given an assignment. An assignment to be a messenger. To let others know about the challenges for families with children who are differently abled. A voice against the inequities of certain insurance policies. An activator to create a place and a program where families can be accepted into the arts community and tell their stories. And now that I've been able to understand that component of the assignment, there just may be a day coming when I might get to play a small part in every newly identified child with hearing loss in this country receiving hearing technology, regardless of loopholes and insurance wiggling.

I'm guessing there's something that's been banging around in your heart. Something that somebody should do something about. Sister Somebody, I'm looking at you. *You.* You can make a huge difference. Pray that God reveals the right season. Pray for God to connect you in the right ways. Pray for courage. And step out there.

**What is that need you've discovered, that pain you've uncovered, that thing you've been saying "somebody should do something" about?**

**Would you say this is something you have a burden for? And by *burden* I mean that it's a need or a topic that keeps showing up on your radar, that keeps a fire lit in your heart.**

We'll sometimes get fired up about something, but we're over it within the next news cycle. But I'm just betting there is something, *something* you've felt a weight for that just might be the thing it's time to stop hoping *They* do something about.

Let's get clear on what being a messenger in this situation is and is not. It is *not* posting scalding opinions on Facebook. It *is* interfacing with people who are directly impacted. It is *not* setting meetings with people you perceive to have power and then dumping the assignment in their laps. It is *not* hiding behind a computer keyboard. It *is* taking steps, even small ones.

**What is a small step you could actively take this week to bring a message of hope to a situation you are concerned about?**

**Have you ever found yourself frustrated with your church, thinking that someone in leadership should fix something or provide something or change something?**

**Read James 1:2-5. What does James say we should do when we experience things that seem unfair—when we encounter frustration or inequity or hurt?**

So, truth-telling time for me: I forget, in my concern and hurt and outrage at certain events, that I can pray for wisdom. Wisdom about next steps. Wisdom about how to intervene. Wisdom that contains God's ideas for helping and healing and honoring. James says that we are being given an opportunity to develop perseverance, which leads us to great maturity, and that God will show up with the information and innovation we need.

**Check out Ephesians 4:11-12. What does it say the role of those in church positions is? What is their primary aim and purpose?**

Did you catch it? Those in vocational ministry, according to Paul, are there to *help* equip us to serve and do good works. Us. Should those in vocational ministry also be doing good works and serving? Absolutely. But at our healthiest, we Christians should be looking to become ever better equipped for the purpose of serving others, not leaning on an institution or an organizational flow chart to make that happen. That's one of the beautiful messages about the body of Christ: We're not waiting on permission to go change the world. He told us to just go do it.

What about you? What holds you back when it comes to making a difference in the things that are important to you? Is it fear? Identify what that fear is. Is it a sense of not having the resources you need? Have you prayed about that? Is it the feeling that you don't know enough about it? If you have access to Wi-Fi and a computer, you can become well educated on just about anything.

**Identify below those things that hold you back; then go one step further and jot down a possible solution or two for each hindrance.**

**Hindrance**                               **Possible Solutions**

**Luke says that Joanna helped support the ministry of Jesus through her own means. Why do you think God had his Son**

rely on the generosity of disciples? He could have sent Him into a wealthy family with a robust network and plenty of resources. Some would say the Christian cause could have spread more quickly that way. What are your thoughts?

*Now you are the body of Christ, and each one of you is a part of it.*
  *1 Corinthians 12:27*

Read 1 Corinthians 12:27 in the margin, focusing on the last section of the verse. Who is part of the body?

To me, James 2:16 seems to be the very clarifying definition for when we confuse the church as *They* instead of we. Write the verse here:

Acts 6:1-4 presents an interesting approach. In our church culture today, there is sometimes an assumption that church ministers and staff should be responsible for meeting physical needs and benevolence requests within the community. Read the passage and record below how early church structure worked:

How does that strike you? Do you think that church ministers or staff should be responsible for meeting these kinds of needs or for empowering others to step into these assignments?

## Beyond Your Church Life

We've focused on the way we sometimes confuse the role of the church when it comes to addressing the needs we see around us. But we also take that expectation of *They* into other marketplaces, with an expectation that government officials and big companies should fix things. And, too often, we allow ourselves to believe that just one woman, or a small group of women, can't carry a message that will bring real change.

But we can! We just have to start somewhere. Maybe you're concerned about the lack of school supplies and support for that elementary school just down the road from you. Don't wait for permission from some *They*. Ask your friends and neighbors to each contribute a box of crayons and a children's book. Whether that ends up being just a handful of supplies you take to the school or you find yourself with the back of your minivan full, you've done it. You've been the messenger. You've carried the burden of your heart into the light of day, and you have made a difference.

Be empowered and emboldened. We sometimes shortchange ourselves before we ever start because we're worried that we won't be heard, that we won't be taken seriously. But that's part of what I love in the story of Joanna and the women of her sisterhood: They didn't try to convince, persuade, or cajole the disciples into believing them. They were simply faithful to tell them what they had experienced and then let that seed embed where it would.

Most important, as believers in Jesus we all are on the same assignment as the messenger Joanna. We all are tasked with sharing with others our experience of finding the tomb empty, of following a Jesus who conquered death. Have you been leaving that assignment up to the experts? You don't have to preach a sermon. You don't have to write a Bible study. You don't have to do a deep dive into ancient Hebrew and Greek scripts. Joanna and the girls didn't run some forensics analysis of the tomb scene. They didn't worry over their verbiage. They simply delivered the message they had been given to deliver: that Jesus is who He says He is.

In all of our social causes and fund-raising and change making, may we never forget that the message of a Jesus who died for us and was raised again is the primary assignment of our lives to a world in which injustices and lack and decay swirl.

**What responsibility do you think you have in being a messenger of the life you have received in Christ? Have you felt that it's something best left to the professionals? Explain your response.**

**When has God opened up opportunities for you to share your faith? Are you more comfortable sharing what you perceive to be the rules of your faith than the experience of your faith? Are you pretty bold when it comes to sharing about your relationship with the Lord, or is it difficult for you?**

**Do you have people in your life right now who need to hear that Jesus was raised from the dead and brings us new life? If so, name them here:**

**With whom do you find it most difficult to talk about faith?**

## Carry the Message

What if?

What if Joanna and the girls had decided that they weren't qualified to let the apostles know about the empty tomb? What if she decided that she couldn't compromise her husband's important position by making such an outlandish claim? What if she had decided to leave the interpretation of that rolled-away stone to the "experts," the Roman officials who had overseen Jesus's execution, the Pharisees, and the sealing of the tomb?

It seems to me that God can always make a way for His purposes and will to be realized. After all, the prophet Isaiah tells us about our God,

> I make known the end from the beginning,
>> from ancient times, what is still to come.
> I say, "My purpose will stand,
>> and I will do all that I please." (Isaiah 46:10)

But Joanna and the girls would have been the ones who missed out. Missed out on who got to have the honor to be the first ones to carry the message of the risen Christ. Missed out on who got to see the disbelief of the apostles turn to awe-inspired conviction about a Messiah who conquered death. Missed out on ushering in a new appreciation and inclusion of women in the faith experience.

Those assignments that God brings to you and me—I pray that we will not try to reassign them. May we receive them with open arms. Even when we feel ill-equipped. Even when we don't fully understand how to make it happen. Even when the world would tell us we're "just" women.

As we wrap up our time looking into Joanna, this Footnote messenger, let's take a little time for confessional prayer journaling:

**God, I thank You that You have made me aware of (fill in a need/injustice/problem you are concerned about)**

_____.

Father, forgive me that I have thought it was someone else's responsibility to take action on this. Forgive me for (fill in how you have moved away from taking action)

_____.

God, I confess that I have allowed (fill in what has held you back) _____ to hold me back as a messenger for you.

Father, I ask for Your help and Your direction in taking active steps to let the world know of Your risen Son, and in exercising mercy, compassion, and charity for those around me.

God, I commit to (fill in the next step you will take in fulfilling your responsibility as a messenger)

_____.

Father, may this be for Your glory alone.
In the name of Jesus, Amen.

## *Joanna*
## The Messenger

*We can serve as God's messengers by sharing what God has done for us and embracing what it means to be the church.*

### Welcome/Prayer/Icebreaker (5-10 minutes)

Welcome to Session 2 of *Footnotes*! This week we're exploring what Joanna has to teach us about what it means to share your faith with others and actively participate in the work God is doing in the world. Take a moment to open with prayer, and then go around the circle and name a time in your life when you felt the Lord was calling you to deliver a message or do something that seemed crazy, odd, or beyond your comfort zone.

### Video (about 20 minutes)

Play the "Getting Started: A Devotional Reflection" video (optional), taking a couple of minutes to focus your hearts and minds on God's Word. Then play the video segment for Session 2, filling in the main idea as you watch and making notes about anything that resonates with you or that you want to be sure to remember.

---

## —Video Notes—

**Scripture:** Luke 24:1-11; Luke 8:1-3

**Main Idea:** Ask not what the _____ can do for you; ask what _____ can do as the church.

**Other Insights:**

---

## Group Discussion (20-25 minutes for a 60-minute session; 30-35 minutes for a 90-minute session)

### Video Discussion

- How would you describe what Jesus has done for you? Who in your circle of influence might need to hear that message? In what ways can you be the church in your world?

### Workbook Discussion

- What is your faith background? How did that shape the way you viewed church? Do you tend to think of church as a place or an organization outside of yourself?
- When a need arises, some people like to thoroughly investigate the situation and make a plan, while others tend to jump straight into action. Both responses are valid. Which approach do you tend to take? How does that impact the way you serve others?
- How do you long to experience church? What do you think your responsibilities are as the church?
- Read Luke 8:1-3. What details stand out to you from this passage? (page 38) How do you think the backgrounds and experiences of these women led them to support the ministry of Jesus and "being" the church? What does this passage say about their motivations and their actions?
- Why do you think it was women to whom the incredible revelation that Jesus had risen from the dead was first given? (page 44)
- Read Mark 16:9-10. Do you sometimes find that you would be willing to be a messenger of the good news of Jesus but then reconsider, worried that people won't believe you? (page 45) What does Joanna's story have to say about this?
- When has God opened up opportunities for you to share your faith? Are you more comfortable sharing what you perceive to be the rules of your faith than the experience of your faith? Are you pretty bold when it comes to sharing about your relationship with the Lord, or is it difficult for you? (page 54)
- Read 1 Corinthians 12:27, focusing on the last section of the verse. Who is part of the body? (page 52) What strengths or abilities do you think you bring to the body of Christ? Do you have an outlet for using those right now?
- Read aloud James 2:16. What role does this tell us we should be playing in what God is doing in the world?

**One to One (10-15 minutes, 90-minute session only)**

Divide into groups of 2-3 and discuss the following:

- What is that need you've discovered, that thing you've been saying "somebody should do something" about? Is it a need or a topic that keeps showing up on your radar, that keeps a fire lit in your heart? What is a small step you could actively take this week to bring a message of hope to a situation you are concerned about? (page 50)

**Closing Prayer (5 minutes)**

Close the session by sharing personal prayer requests and praying together. In addition to praying out loud for one another, ask God to help you be bold in living out your faith through words and actions. Pray for the courage to go when He directs you.

# Week 3

## Epaphras

### The Wrestler

---

# 1

---

*The art of living is more like wrestling than dancing.*

Marcus Aurelius, *Meditations*

## Wrestling—for Real

My husband, Michael, has some serious matriarchs in his line. These ancestral girls came to play. Heavens. And one of the most fascinating to me is Michael's maternal great-grandmother, Maudie Mae Spencer. There are all kinds of amazing stories surrounding her, from forcing a hardscrabble living from dusty farms to surviving a house explosion while pregnant with her ninth child. We've got this amazing anthology of grainy pictures documenting her ninety-three-year-long life, from a slightly blurred black-and-white photo from 1914 showing Maudie in a bonnet and long prairie dress outside her farmhouse with a few of her children, pregnant belly pushing against the calico print of her dress, to some of the last snapshots taken of her in the early 1980s, hair in a white cloud of nonagenarian curls and a grin as big as the Oklahoma sky.

After she turned ninety, the family decided it was time for her to hang up her plow. Literally. She had continued to plow her own garden well into her ninth decade of life, pushing the old relic through red Oklahoma dirt, carving straight lines into the soil, ready for seeds. Mike loved going to visit her in her little house in Haskell (a suburb of Muskogee, Oklahoma, if Muskogee considered itself snooty enough to have a suburb, which it doesn't). Trinkets of her long life were anchored on lacy doilies, and plastic covers protected the upholstered furniture. Yet, should you veer into a mental image of a sugar-sweet great-grandmother in a cookie-perfumed house, let me lift that from you and insert instead the main activity that Michael and his great-grandmother would share.

When Michael visited, she would have him sit alongside her on her ancient yet pristine sofa, click on the television, turn the knob to the appointed channel, adjust the antenna, and they would sit back and watch . . . wrestling. And I'm talking the kind of wrestling with all the crazy costumes and hype and drama. "It's real!" she would insist to Michael. She knew all the contenders, all the interpersonal intrigues and previous matches and the grudges held by the outcomes of those matches.

I just love the juxtaposition of that darling little old lady hollering at the television, her great-grandson beside her, fully engaged in the ringside pageantry. Now, I'm not here to debate if that type of wrestling is real or not, fiction or fantasy or fierce. What I think is important here is that Maudie Mae stayed in the game, so to speak. She was still engaged in combat, wanting to see the virtuous and the good vanquishing evil.

Given her love for wrestlers, I think Maudie Mae would have loved our Footnote this week—a man named Epaphras (pronounced EP-a-fras).[1] Epaphras was Paul's trusted friend, confidant, and ministry partner. He's only mentioned three times in Scripture, but we see painted there a picture of someone who was faithful, who was trusted, and who was passionate about serving the church.

We learn that Epaphras struggled and engaged. Paul doesn't just say Epaphras prayed. He doesn't just say Epaphras prayed *a lot*. Paul is very intentional to tell us the intensity Epaphras brought to praying—that he was "always wrestling" (Colossians 4:12). And Paul is clear that the prayers of Epaphras were specific, as he prayed that these baby Christians in the faith would stand firm in the will of God.

Let's face it, there are plenty of amazing books on the practice of prayer, and all kinds of ideas out there on how to pray, when to pray, what to pray for. I won't even pretend I have the kind of prayer life that would make me a contender to write one of those kinds of books. Prayer is something I've had to fight for, that I've had to make a consistent part of my life, that I've had to analyze and deconstruct and rebuild what role it plays in my life. So I won't even pretend that we'll walk through these lessons and come out the other side with a neat template for you to model.

But what we will do is think about the prayer life of this Footnote, Epaphras, and glean from those quick words attributed to his memory what it means to wrestle in prayer, and what we can learn, not about the "how" of prayer, but the "'why'" that goes beyond us.

How engaged are we in the struggles, the wrestlings of those around us? Of the plight of others in countries where freedom of faith isn't a thing? For those we want to see come to faith in Christ, or for the strengthening and deepening of the faith walks of those who will be the next generation of the church, that they would stand firm in the will of God? Or do we spend our time "wrestling" on Facebook, spouting our opinions and shock over social issues rather than taking our concerns and requests and fears and questions to the Lord in prayer? So, what does it mean to take something "to the mat" in prayer?

**Let's take a look at the three places in Scripture where that wrestling champ Epaphras is mentioned. Take note of what you find there that gives you clues about Epaphras.**

**Colossians 1:6-7**

**Colossians 4:12**

**Philemon 23**

**Now, let's go back to the first chapter in Colossians. What exactly is it that the church at Colossae had first learned from Epaphras, as Paul says in 1:6-7?**

*Epaphras, who is one of you and a servant of Christ Jesus, sends greetings. He is always wrestling in prayer for you, that you may stand firm in all the will of God, mature and fully assured.*

Colossians 4:12

**What are the adjectives Paul uses to describe Epaphras in Colossians 1:7?**

**What do you think Paul means in Colossians 4:12 when he calls Epaphras "one of you"?**

Scholars think that Epaphras was originally from Colossae, a small city known for its cool streams that ran through the woods outside of town. It wasn't a major trade center or a city set on an important trade route. It was something of a backwater kind of a place.

**In Philemon 23, what does Paul call Epaphras?**

Epaphras actually visited Paul in prison in Rome. A quick search on Google Maps gives a whole lot more context to this undertaking. If you have computer access, go to the navigation site of your choice and find out how far Colossae is from Rome. I'll do a bit of the math for you: Colossae is 2,098 kilometers from Rome, which is 1,304 miles. Um, yeah. That means that Epaphras had to go even further than the distance from Los Angeles to Dallas to visit Paul in prison. No Uber. No Southwest.

**What does it tell you about Epaphras's character and relationship with Paul that he would undertake such a journey?**

**Which descriptions would you assign to Epaphras, based on what we know from Scripture? Circle your choices.**

Devoted

Distracted

Committed

Flighty

Enduring

Demanding

Persevering

Temperamental

Courageous

Patient

Epaphras was willing to hang on to and grapple with those needs of the early church through prayer, with a tenacity that is rare. We can admire that kind of prayer commitment; we can aspire to it. But it can be oh-so-hard to emulate. Throughout our study this week we're going to consider five things that keep us from taking our concerns consistently to the prayer mat.

## We Have Commitment Issues

The first obstacle to persistent prayer has to do with commitment. We live in an age where we are somewhat commitment phobic. In my tenure as a women's pastor it has been quite an experience in faith and frustration as we put together events for our home church and region. People just have a tough time committing to get their plans made and their tickets purchased until the last minute. While I accept it's just part of our culture now, it does make it challenging to plan and budget well.

We also see it in volunteer ranks for various events. People commit to a certain area of service and then bail right before. Or people don't sign up to help, then contact us right before an event, ready to jump in. While we are certainly blessed with a great core of people who invest their time and heart and service consistently, that last minute opt-in or opt-out commitment crew adds a layer of complexity.

As a generation, we seem to be getting, dare I say it, flaky. Flaky is becoming the norm. I'm not trying to throw anybody under the bus. But we do need to understand that some of the things that will bring us robust spiritual maturity and peace require diligence. Duty. Discipline. Those concepts aren't too popular these days, but their value remains.

There are so many choices and events and experiences to be had today. There are so many diversions and last-minute options. Our schedules are packed, our interests are broad, our attentions are distracted. We hate to commit to something just in case something more interesting comes along. Or we try to cram too much into our time constraints. That's probably the area where I can come off as flaky—I overcommit with our crazy family schedule, a project at work takes a little longer than expected, the dentist's office is running behind, and *boom*! I'm canceling and rescheduling and apologizing all over the place.

And I can be the same way with the spiritual disciplines of my life.

I was going to go to that small group, but this other thing came up.

I was going to get through the whole Bible this year. But then that next installment of that best-selling fiction series I've been waiting for finally came out and, well . . .

I meant to pray each day for that friend of mine going through a hard time. But I lost that sticky note with her name on it.

I'm not finger pointing here, sisters. I'm confessing.

But oh. Prayer.

There is a call to stay in prayer. To continue. To wrestle. To stay in the discipline. To not flake out, give up, or be distracted when the heavens seem silent and the future distant. To wrestle. To wrestle well.

I have this sense that maybe some of the prayers we've prayed aren't unanswered prayers; maybe they were unwrestled prayers. God presented us with an opportunity to lean deeply into Him and we did—for a moment. But then we got distracted or frustrated and we exited the prayer closet. And that unwrestled prayer was left suspended.

What of this? What if, sometimes, we're just flat offering flaky prayers? No depth, no nutritional value, just something that tickles the tongue and satisfies the senses, but makes no mark, leaves no imprint. We toss prayers, just to say we've uttered them. I'm guilty. You may be too. Someone asks me to pray about the job decision they're trying to make, the doctor's visit they have next week, the learning challenge their child is experiencing. And I do pray. But so often, more than I'd like to confess, I'm tossing that prayer up to God, rather than wrestling it down in faith. I'm lofting up fly balls of requests, hoping God will field them. But I'm praying from the wrong metaphor. To wrestle requires losing the fluff, deflating the air, and digging in.

**Read John 17. Here Jesus is praying for His disciples' futures. What stands out to you in His prayer?**

**What can you apply from His example in your prayers for the generations to come?**

In Romans 15:4 there's a word that speaks to diligence, to tenacity. In the New International Version, it's the word *endurance*. In the original Greek it's two words, *hypomonē* and *paraklēsis*, which mean to abide and to beg, to call for help.[2] To abide in a place of seeking God's intervention and help . . . sounds like wrestling prayer to me.

**Read Romans 15:4 in the margin. What does Paul say the purpose of what was written in the past is?**

*For everything that was written in the past was written to teach us, so that through the endurance taught in the Scriptures and the encouragement they provide we might have hope.*

*Romans 15:4*

**Is it possible that you have some *unwrestled* prayers out there, prayers that you thought were unanswered but now you're beginning to wonder? Would you be willing to wrestle afresh in prayer? Why or why not?**

**Read Luke 2:36-38. Who had been fasting and praying? For how long?**

Sometimes people pray for the restoration of a relationship, a dream, a joy, a life. But as time passes, it seems they can't move on. Some would say they are standing firm in faith. Others would say they are living in denial. At times it can be really hard to tell the difference.

For some of us, we've wrestled. Boy, have we. And apparently God's will doesn't line up with what we've wrestled for. When I speak, I sometimes talk about the challenges two of my girls have faced—my daughter Maesyn, who has hearing loss, and my daughter Merci, who experienced a stroke at birth. We've wrestled in prayer for those girls—for healing and for their roads to be easier. But for whatever reason, God has allowed the hearing loss and the aftereffects of the stroke to remain. It was after speaking at an event recently and talking about the girls that I received an interesting email from someone who had been in attendance. This person, in what I'm sure she thought was love, told me that I needed to reevaluate my understanding of God; that God would never allow these issues to exist in my girls' lives. This person went on to tell me that I needed more faith-filled prayer for my girls to be healed, having full expectation. She frankly chastised me for not believing big enough, not praying often enough, and not praying with enough authority. She was assuming we hadn't done those things.

But we had wrestled. We had believed big. We had.

When we talk about wrestlng in prayer, we want to be cautious not to confuse dedication to prayer and the outcome. Wrestling has value, whether things turn out the way we would like or not. After all, one of the strongest examples of prayer wrestling we see in Scripture is Jesus wrestling in the garden of Gethsemane right before He is arrested. He wrestles to the point of sweating blood, asking that the events that were looming before Him might not have to take place. But in the end, Jesus gives us the ultimate example when He prays these incredible words, "Yet not my will, but yours be done" (Luke 22:42).

The important part is that I continue to wrestle for my girls—to wrestle for the impact they will have on the world; to wrestle for the unique journeys God has them on; to wrestle for the lives they will influence and the reach they will have *because* of the challenges they have faced.

**What do you think the difference is between a wrestling prayer and a denial of what is? How can you tell the difference?**

**Have you had a time you have wrestled in prayer? If so, describe it.**

*Rejoice always,
pray continually,
give thanks in all
circumstances; for
this is God's will for
you in Christ Jesus.*
*1 Thessalonians
5:16-18*

**Read 1 Thessalonians 5:16-18 in the margin. What do you think it means to pray continually? What might it look like for you to pray continually?**

I want to challenge you to take up this wrestling of prayers not as a hobby but as a decision to go pro. And the difference between having a passing hobby and truly engaging in a practice that defines you and shapes how you spend your time is *time*. I'm not talking about committing an hour a day to prayer. I am talking about picking two or three issues that you are going to press into, that you are going to bring up in prayer again and again and again.

And then again.

**Write the issues you want to commit to prayer here:**

If we have wrestled in prayer and have been disappointed by the outcome, sometimes we can be hesitant to enter the ring again. Or if we have wrestled in prayer and have seen mountains move, sometimes we think we've cracked the code and can expect God to fulfill our every petition. May we move to the place that we are willing to wrestle simply because we encounter God there, and in the encountering may we learn to hear Him and lean more fully into His will.

# 2

*"A bird doesn't sing because it has an answer,*
*it sings because it has a song."*

Joan Walsh Anglund, A *Cup of Sun* (1967)

## We Think Prayer Won't Make a Difference

A second obstacle to persistent prayer has to do with our impatience.

A few years ago, Mike needed to go to a business conference at a pretty swank resort and I got to tag along. (Really tough, but somebody had to do it!) We went to a beautiful spot outside of Phoenix, Arizona, to a place called Boulders. From the gorgeous landscaping to the incredible weather and beautiful food, it was a fantastic trip. Mike was in back-to-back meetings most of the day, so I had some time to read, run, and wander. Off to one side of the resort was a hiking trail that led up into the craggy cliffs overlooking the valley, so I hit the trail and climbed. The view was amazing, but I found something secretive in the cliffs that was even more amazing to me.

The native peoples who originally inhabited that valley lived among the rocky overhangs in the cliffs, and it was there that I found their kitchen—a series of boulders upon which generations had ground corn and grain and, in doing so, had carved out grinding bowls in the rock. Over the years, through diligence, daily-ness, and duty, they literally marked into the rock the mark of their existence,

As I sat there under the rock overhang, I put my hands into the grinding holes and thought of the meals prepared there. They had wrestled the rock into a place of sustenance. Sheer rock. And through persistence, they were able to mold that rock into a tool, a place to render kernels to bread. And now, centuries later, the work of that persistence remains. There are bowls carved into the rocks, bowls that held sustenance.

Sometimes we're impatient with our prayers, thinking they aren't making a difference. Early in my faith walk, I prayed just because the Bible said we were supposed to. And I didn't want to tick God off because, of what I was told of Him, He seemed to be pretty easily angered. So I prayed because it was something that was on the list of to-dos to keep me in good standing with God. But I had also been taught that He didn't really do much with those prayers. He didn't interfere much with the dramas and foibles and little worries of humankind. He'd gotten the planet spinning and the system set up, and then He needed to head out on some other celestial business trips; He'd come back at some point and get our report cards and assign us to heaven or hell. I was taught to pray to stay on God's good side.

In my twenties, as I began to seek a relationship with God of my own, I took a fresh look at prayer and its implications. And I got to know a whole group of Christians who had a decidedly different take on prayer. They were pretty sure they had figured out a way to get God to do anything they wanted, if they just used the right prayer formula and the right verbiage and the right intensity of faith and emotion. It was a one-eighty from what I had known, from not expecting God to ever really answer to putting Him on a timetable that He was honor-bound to respond to in a timely manner because all the secret protocols and postures had been used.

I wrestled with those two extremes.

And then, as we always should, I went back to the Word—and checked the math.

I read that we have twenty-five examples of Jesus praying in Scripture. The apostle Paul mentions prayer forty-one times. And there are about 650 prayers throughout the Old and New Testaments. And catch this: 450 of those prayers were answered in Scripture.[3] That means 200 were not answered, at least as recorded in the Bible. So about 70 percent of the prayers recorded in the Bible were answered and about 30 percent were not—at least as far as being recorded for posterity goes.

Hmm. What to do with stats like that?

For me, it stands as a reminder that, yes, we pray for today. And we *also* pray for what we might not get to see fulfilled in our lifetimes. It changes the way I pray, to be contending not only for those current issues in my life and in the lives of others but also for those to come. To wrestle for them.

I want to be the kind of woman who, as generations pass and some-one comes across the boulders of my faith life, they will find proof that I ground out prayers, that I wrestled the rock. I want them to be able to stand there, place their hands in the bowls that held those prayers, and look out on a landscape that is changed because I dared to contend for them.

**Take a moment to pray for your great-great-grandchildren, or for the great-great-grandchildren of a close friend. For people who haven't even been born yet. What would you pray over them? What kind of faith would you wrestle for them to have? What would you ask God to help them stand firm for?**

**Read Hebrews 11:13-16. (And, really, you should just knock out the whole chapter. It's amazing.) What do you learn about the faith giants and what was fulfilled in their lifetimes?**

**Do you find that the majority of your prayer life is about the immediate, the critical, the urgent? If so, why do you think that is? (If you're like me, that's when you most "remember" to pray.)**

**How can you make praying for what is *important*, not just what is imminent, part of your time with God?**

**What are some other things the Holy Spirit brings to mind that you could be praying forward?**

We may not always get answers or the answers we seek when we pray, but we do receive fresh perspective. We may not always like the circumstances from which spring some of our most painful prayers, but we will receive peace. And we may struggle with continuing to pray over things that don't seem to be changing or that remain confusing, but we develop perseverance in the doing. So, yes, pray with faith. Pray and listen. And also receive perspective, peace, and perseverance.

## We Forget to Pray

A third obstacle to persistent prayer has to do with forgetfulness.

For several years now, we've been sponsoring a child through Compassion International. They make it simple to do, and allow you to automate sending support to the child you sponsor. In our busy lives, I appreciate the convenience of making sure I'm getting those sponsorship dollars sent his way, taking care of his medical, educational, and nutritional needs. But here's where I've blown it. Because the most basic aspect of our sponsorship is automated, I've often failed to remain intentional in doing the one thing that is most essential for this darling boy, beyond whatever material resources I have to share with him. I often forget to wrestle for him in prayer.

I've kept his picture on our fridge as a reminder, but then when the kitchen was being repainted and everything was pulled off the refrigerator and stuffed in a drawer, I didn't get his picture put back in its accustomed place. I've also kept his picture in my planner, but then I switched day planner strategies and am keeping all those appointments on my phone calendar. And even when I had his picture on the fridge and in my day planner, I still hadn't committed to making a discipline out of my wrestling for him. Those visual reminders helped, sure, but they were in happenstance places, not a consistent place I commit to going to every day. Making an elaborate prayer board or shellacking the interior of a prayer closet with printouts of verses and reminders is lovely, but won't do a thing for you if you don't actually make it a discipline to get your eyes on it every day or enter that prayer closet consistently. (I can get so much more excited about putting a project together than actually then utilizing the outcome of that project.)

While I don't ever want to take my prayer wrestling routine to the point that it just becomes something I repeat without thought, there is something powerful about creating a routine for yourself that takes you in a consistent way to that wrestling mat. For me, it's a series of steps and people I wrestle for in prayer in a certain order at the same time each day. I have specific things I'm praying about for them. I start with my oldest child and the specific prayer I have for her right now. I say her name and give my request to God. Then I move on to my second child and what I am wrestling for her right now. And then my third child. And fourth. And fifth. And sixth. And seventh. And eighth. I then lift up my husband by name and the definitive item I am wrestling for him. Then my brothers and their families. Then other members of our extended family. Then my church family. It gives me a thoughtful cadence by which I make a discipline of my wrestling.

We have a tradition at our church that we engage every two or three years. On a Sunday, our pastor will have a sticky note passed out to each person in the congregation and he'll have us each put a name on that sticky note, a person whom we are committing to pray for during a set number of days. We then take those sticky notes and stick them across the front apron of our stage, where they remain for all the days we've committed to praying. As a staff, we take time throughout the week to go to the sanctuary and pray over all those thousands of sticky notes. It's powerful. It's a strong visual about the needs represented within our faith community. And it's an incredible reminder to not forget about those who need our prayers, who need our wrestling.

**What are some things you can do to help you remember to wrestle in prayer? Consider the following ideas and add a few of your own—things that will serve as reminders to keep that issue or person you're praying for very much on your dashboard as you seek to wrestle on behalf of the people you love.**

- **A timer set on your phone to go off at specific intervals as a reminder to pray for someone**
- **Pictures placed in your car, on your phone, or in other places you frequent as a reminder**

- **A prayer journal, either in a notebook or on the notes app on your phone, where you jot down prayer items**

**Other ideas:**

## We Have Stereotypes About Prayer

A fourth obstacle to persistent prayer has to do with stereotypes.

I'm always struggling a bit with watching how other people do things and then thinking that's exactly how I need to do it, specifically in areas where I feel like I'm not as talented. I can be a bit of a bold maverick when it comes to forging my own way in certain areas, but there are other areas where the awkward, self-conscious me shows up in spades.

When I was in high school, I would study how the cool girl in my class did her hair and would pepper her with all kinds of questions about how exactly she got her wings to feather like that (where are my girls who remember feathered hair?). In retrospect, that classmate might have found me a bit stalkerish. I've done the same thing with how to decorate my home or how to organize. These are areas I've struggled in, and so I figure that someone else's recipe must be the best.

I've also been fascinated with how people walk out their spiritual practices. I've looked for templates and schedules and resources that seem to be so successful for others, and then I've attempted to copy and paste them into my own life. If so-and-so seems to have some kind of superhero spiritual life, if they are "more" in whatever area I feel "less," well then, let's unpack how they do this God thing and apply it to my own life.

Listen. It is helpful to learn from others' experiences and personal disciplines; that's a good thing. By doing so, we can save ourselves some time, learn powerful insights, break some new ground, and make some progress when we are humble and seek counsel and guidance and model what we find there. But too often we can be tempted to take what has been hard won and customized in someone else's life and assume it's the way we must do it, regardless of the way God has knit us together, regardless of the spiritual gifts He's bestowed on us and the purpose He has in mind.

I've done that with prayer.

I've got those friends who get up at the crack of dawn. They make

that soothing cup of organic herbal tea in the artisan mug they got on that last mission trip to South America. They slide into that comfortable chair set in their prayer corner, a tidy basket of items on the marble-top side table beside them, dainty Kleenexes and favorite writing pens and their tapestry-covered Bible in close reach. And then they embark on their one-hour commitment to quiet time and prayer, so engaged and focused in their time with God that they have to set a reminder alarm on their phone to remind them to wind up and go gently wake their children for the upcoming day.

Y'all. How I wish. How I wish I could tell you that's my kind of prayerful wrestling. But given that this is a Bible study, I should be honest here, shouldn't I? If I'm up at the crack of dawn, it's because I'm frantically pushing toward a book deadline or I've got an early morning flight booked to go speak. Otherwise, you'll find me trying to squeeze every second out of my sleep quotient. That comfy chair in a solitary corner idea? Every chair in my house is in a state of constant rearranging and questionable upholstery with the mass of humanity we have through here on a daily basis. And if there are any items like Kleenexes and good pens in a basket, they will not stay there for long. (You should hear some of the hissy fits I throw over scissors disappearing and the kids taking my highlighters. The struggle is real.)

And aside from all that household reality, there's this: I'm at my most connected to God when I'm moving. Creating. Running. Driving. Or in a hot bathtub at the end of the day. I've spent a fair amount of time beating myself up about not being one of those still, quiet, early-bird morning pray-ers. I watch a movie like *War Room* and then I beat myself up some more because I love the idea of a prayer closet. And I can barely get in any of the closets in this house, much less clear one to become Prayer Central. So I'd need to have a team of professional organizers come dig out my closets so I could even begin to designate one as a war room.

But in all of that, I was missing the point again. I was confusing the activities surrounding the habit of prayer with actually praying. The habits and locales and clocks of some people I admire when it comes to their prayer lives distract me from the main thing.

The main thing is to pray. I mean, duh. But really. To make prayer your habit. And to embrace who God created you to be, the way He designed you, and put that to work to design a prayer life in which you are able to pray from a place of habit and consistency. To take whatever habit works for you and to make it the wrestling mat on which you meet those things you're praying about. And to wrestle them thoroughly in prayer.

Running is a really important prayer closet for me. Sometimes it's outside, asphalt grinding beneath my feet. Sometimes it's on a tread-mill when the weather turns bad, and I'll take sticky notes of the prayer requests of the women I minister to, plastering them on the wall in front of my treadmill, each stride, each mile a prayer. When my physical body is focused on trying to churn out the next mile, something happens in my mind and spirit that allows me to focus on talking with God—and listening. We tend to forget that important component, don't we? Prayer is, yes, about making our requests known to God, about telling Him our fears and concerns, about praising Him. But it's also about taking the time to listen.

Far too often, I've evaluated my spiritual disciplines based on how "sweet" they have seemed. But maybe, just maybe, for some of us, it's about how spiritually "sweaty" we get instead of "sweet." I've been too quick to discount those experiences or judge my time with God because it hasn't matched the admirable sweet, quiet times of women I admire.

But who says how it should be? Jesus takes a nap in a storm-tossed boat and then calms the waves. He prays and wrestles in a dark garden of Gethsemane, under a haunting moon. Paul prays with might in the throes of a storm that takes down a ship. He is found loudly singing at midnight in a prison cell. Wrestling is a full-contact sport that can, yes, take place in the solitude of a quiet morning or in the chaos of the eve-ning rush hour. Daniel was one of the early-bird types who everyone knew the exact spot and time of day he would be praying, which is amazing. But all we know about Epaphras's prayer life is the most important thing we need to know—that he wrestled and grappled with and labored over those baby Christians in Colossae, not just for their immediate needs, but for the church that would be. It was what Epaphras was wrestling *for*, not the mechanics necessarily of how he was doing that.

**What have you typically defined as the elements of a successful quiet time, or prayer time, before God? Think about the things you have made part of that definition and write them below.**

**When do you feel most connected to God? What works for you when it comes to prayer? Do you need the quiet and stillness**

**because that's how He created you? Or do you prefer to pray in a different way and place? Are you a night owl or a morning bird?**

**Whose prayer life or spiritual life have you admired and desired to model? What about their disciplines has appealed to you? As you reflect on your answers to the questions about what works for you, are their spiritual habits a good fit for you?**

I want you to be encouraged that the God who knit you together—you, with your ability to deeply focus, or you, the one who often gets curious and distracted—knows who you are. He just wants you to talk to Him. If that's in a very traditional prayer environment, awesome. If it's while you're Rollerblading back to the house after dropping off your kids at school, awesome. (I'll be praying for you, too, if you're Rollerblading, because wheels and sidewalks . . . yikes!) Drop the stereotypes you may be carrying around for prayer, embrace who He created you to be, and get to it. And watch things change.

---

# 3

---

*Certain things simply will not happen without the operation of prayer.*

Elisabeth Elliot, A *Lamp Unto My Feet* (2004)

## We Get Prayer and Study Confused

A fifth obstacle to persistent prayer has to do with confusion about what prayer is.

Do you know there is a difference in studying the Word and in wrestling in prayer? There is. I spend *a lot* of time at a table, at my desk, in the conference room in my church, preparing teachings and writing and doing deep dives into original Greek words and Hebrew history. I have praise and worship music going during that time. Those hours spent studying are a joy to me. I feel close to God, close to His Word. I love the things He shows me, the things I learn. That's not prayer wrestling. Nope. It is needed, and it is a valuable part of my spiritual discipline. But I've finally embraced the difference between study and prayer.

Look, I want you to enjoy your study time. I hope it's a big part of your life. But don't confuse it with prayer, with wrestling for those you love and for those who are to come. And receive permission to use the place and practice for prayer that helps you hear Him best.

I love a story I ran across about D. L. Moody, a Christian evangelist and publisher in the late 1800s. He was an enthusiastic and big personality who was passionate and practical in his faith. The story goes like this:

> It is related that during one of D. L. Moody's Atlantic Ocean crossings a fire broke out in the hold of the ship. A friend is reported to have said to the famous evangelist. "Mr. Moody, let us go to the other end of the ship and engage in prayer." The heavenly-minded yet down-to-earth Moody replied, "Not so, sir; we stand right here and pass buckets and pray hard all the time."[4]

I love that Moody reminds us that we can pray while passing the buckets. Just as going to the other end of the ship would not make prayer any more effective, neither would it be of help to call passing the buckets prayer. Passing the buckets is passing the buckets and praying hard is praying hard.

Sometimes we think time at church counts as prayer. Sometimes we think good deeds count as prayer. Sometimes we think a really emotional and impactful time of praise and worship is prayer. But it's not.

Definitely pass the buckets. But keep on praying too.

**What about prayer is hard for you?**

**Do you tend to consider your time studying the Bible as your time with God? Or do you find that you sometimes prefer doing a Bible study assignment over praying? If so, why do you think that is?**

## What Do You Want Your Spiritual Legacy to Be?

My mother-in-law, Linda Carr, had a catchphrase. A catchphrase is something that a person is known for saying repeatedly, something that becomes part of his or her personal brand, if you will. Virtually every time I wrapped up a conversation with my mother-in-law, whether we had been chatting on the phone or finishing up a lingering time over the breakfast table with a cup of coffee, she would ask, "How can I be praying for you?"

Now, I have to admit, there were times that catchphrase would irritate me a little bit. I might have been keeping an eye on my watch, knowing I needed to hustle out the door to get to the next thing. And I would sometimes just toss out an, "Oh, you know, just making sure I'm doing all the things God wants me to," or something of that nature. It certainly wasn't just with me that my mother-in-law employed this catchphrase. It was all the time, with all kinds of people, in all kinds of settings. It was sweet and sometimes induced a bit of eye-rolling, and it definitely was part of what she was known for.

When Linda died in the spring of 2018, we were stunned. She'd had a medical procedure the year before that had sent her health sideways, but we all thought she was improving, even though her recovery had been difficult. Things suddenly went south, and we found ourselves planning a funeral instead of her next trip to come see us. As we were scrambling to find pictures for Linda's memorial service and important papers, my brother-in-law stumbled across a little red notebook. Inside, in her elementary-school-teacher perfect script, was written line upon line upon line, all those prayer requests she'd collected over all those years of asking that catchphrase, "How can I be praying for you?"

She hadn't just said those words—she'd meant them. She would pray through that notebook on a consistent basis. As prayers were answered,

Linda would put a line through the request with a note about how it was answered. If someone had been praying for healing and they were physically healed, she would jot that down with a scribble of praise. If that physical healing didn't come and someone died, she would put a smiley face and note they were now healed in eternity and with God. From "little" requests to earthshaking ones, it was all there, faithfully recorded.

As we went through her Bible and found more notes, we began to realize more fully what it all meant. She wrestled. Flat-out wrestled for those in her prayer notebooks. For my husband. For my children. For the people she encountered in the store. For her pastor. For the neighbors, the bank teller, people important to her friends. My name is in there many times with those things I would offer in response to her question, "How can I be praying for you?" Even those things I mentioned flippantly. Even those things that gutted me. Even those things I barely remembered. Even those things I'll never forget. All there, recorded and prayed over by a faithful wrestler.

It was more than a catchphrase. It was a commitment.

How can I do anything but stand in awe and gratitude of that legacy? What do you want to be known for? Linda is of the tribe of Epaphras, as far as I'm concerned. I suspect that's the corner of heaven she's frequenting the most, hanging out with fellow wrestlers who pinned doubt and fear to the floor and went to the mat for the people in their lives, those near and dear and those far away.

And now, having found those notebooks of Linda's, it seems fitting that she was the granddaughter of that wrestling fan we read about at the first of this lesson, Maudie Mae.

**What are the catchphrases you are currently known for? (And if you don't know, I'm sure your kids, husband, or coworkers would be more than happy to tell you!)**

**Are those the catchphrases you want to be known for? If not, what changes do you need to make to how you are living out loud to others?**

As we close this week's study, I want you to take some time to truly consider what you would love for people to remember about you when you pass from this life to the next. It's a sobering thing to deeply consider what you want your legacy to be. Take some time with this. Write it down. There's something about writing those kinds of things down that can help make us more intentional.

**What do you hope people will remember about your life and legacy? Include what practices you can begin today to build that faith legacy—prayer by prayer. All the way to the mat.**

## *The Wrestler*

*Our commitment to prayer has lasting impact in the lives of others and for the church.*

### Welcome/Prayer/Icebreaker (5-10 minutes)

Welcome to Session 3 of *Footnotes*! This week we're exploring what Epaphras has to teach us about what it looks like to be committed in prayer. Take a moment to open with prayer, and then go around the circle and ask, *What is an area of your life where you are disiciplined or diligent—somewhere you "wrestle" with commitment?*

### Video (about 20 minutes)

Play the "Getting Started: A Devotional Reflection" video (optional), taking a couple of minutes to focus your hearts and minds on God's Word. Then play the video segment for Session 3, filling in the main idea as you watch and making notes about anything that resonates with you or that you want to be sure to remember.

---

### —Video Notes—

**Scripture:** Colossians 1:7; 4:12; Hebrews 12:1

**Main Idea:** Are we willing in _____ and in _____, like Epaphras, to wrestle . . . for those who come after?

**Other Insights:**

---

## Group Discussion (20-25 minutes for a 60-minute session; 30-35 minutes for a 90-minute session)

### *Video* Discussion

- Have you ever wrestled in prayer for something/someone? Or has someone done that for you? What were the effects of that season of prayer?

### *Workbook* Discussion

- Take turns reading aloud Colossians 1:6-7; Colossians 4:12; and Philemon 23. What do you learn about Epaphras from these verses? (page 63) Which descriptions would you assign to Epaphras based on what we know from Scripture? (page 65)
- What are some prayers that you've seen answered—but it took a long time? Was there a lesson you learned in that time gap?
- Read 1 Thessalonians 5:16-18. What do you think it means to pray continually? (page 69) Are there any ways you've discovered to help you do just that? What effect has that had on your faith journey?
- How willing are you to continue to pray, even when you don't feel like you're seeing answers? Read Psalm 66:17-20; Jeremiah 29:12-13; Philippians 4:6-7; and 1 John 5:15. What encouragement do you find in these verses?
- Which of the five obstacles to prayer that we've considered this week tend to trip you up the most, and why?
- What does it mean to "pray forward"? Do you think today's prayers can make a difference into the future of your friends, your children, and your descendants? Why or why not?
- How does the idea of "wrestling in prayer" strike you? Does it seem repetitive? Does it feel like you are trying to convince God? What do you think the purpose of wrestling in prayer is?
- How can you make praying for what is *important*, not just what is imminent, part of your time with God? (page 73)

## One to One (10-15 minutes, 90-minute session only)

Divide into groups of 2-3 and discuss the following:

- When do you feel most connected to God? What works for you when it comes to prayer? (page 78) What about prayer is hard for you? (page 80)

## Closing Prayer (5 minutes)

Close the session by sharing personal prayer requests and praying together. In addition to praying out loud for one another, ask God for the courage and consistency to come to Him often, confident that He hears you, and for increased faith in the lasting impact of prayer.

# Week 4

## Quirinius

### The Careerist

---

## 1

---

*As long as it is day, we must do the works of him who sent me. Night is coming, when no one can work.*

John 9:4

### Exactly What I Didn't Expect

I was sitting on the couch, half-heartedly climbing my way up yet another summit of Mount Laundry when I heard it—the pitch of my children's voices that signaled to me that conflict and sibling warfare were about to spark. I sighed and heaved my heavily pregnant self up the stairs up to the girls' bedrooms. With each tired step, the intonation of my daughters' voices was growing more frantic, urgent, and frustrated, and I felt that surge of mothering irritation swell. My usual State of the Union address began to form in my thoughts, with emphasis on phrases like "Is this how we treat each other?" and "Does this mean you want to go to bed early tonight?" punctuating my coming intervention. By the time I arrived at the closed bedroom door where the girls were squabbling loudly on the other side, I was ready to pounce and shut down this sisterhood kerfuffle.

With my hand on the doorknob, I paused. Something of a change in one of the girls' voices held me back. And then I listened.

"I never thought my wedding would turn out like this!" one of the girls' voices wailed.

Huh? Okay, wait.

I listened a bit longer through the closed door and heard the pretend voice of another character enter the dialogue. "First the tornado, then the dog eating the cake, and now this!" intoned a somber voice.

Turning the knob quietly and peeking around the edge of the door, I found, not a fistfight about to break out between my girls, but a Barbie wedding in complete disarray. Madison and McKenna were in full character as a wide range of wedding attendees, all in various states of gossip and commentary about what had gone wrong with the nuptials of Barbie and Ken. Barbie Dreamhouse furniture was scattered in front of the Dreamhouse itself, where apparently an outdoor wedding had been underway when things went south. The girls noticed me at some point and began explaining, with great animation and enthusiasm, all the things that had played havoc with the dream wedding. As they talked, they began scheming up new elements to the plot and got ready to reset the entire theater of Barbie-ville, ready to take another stab at sabotaging the next attempt at a wedding.

I'd headed upstairs expecting one thing from the clues I was getting. I was ready to bust in and have a mothering moment, only to wander into something else that was an intentional exploration of the unexpected.

Pretty meta, huh? A lot of adulting has seemed like that to me. I felt like I was served up a whole program as a kid in school that if I would just learn good penmanship, if I could simply master the five-paragraph essay, if I would score high enough on college entrance exams, if I would put in the miles on the track, if I would put in the vocal practice, if I would learn the lines, then success not only was assured but was my right. Never mind that in the middle of trying to do all the right things, I experienced plenty of times of not getting the part, not getting the spot, not making the grade. *It's my fault*, I would think. *I've just got to try harder and get it right and be earlier and fight more ferociously.* And so by the time I hit those early years of adulthood, I was ready for the system to start working the way all those teachers and mentors and inspirational quotes had assured me they would.

Wah-wah-wah. Yeah, that doesn't seem to be how adulting works at all. Or, at least, a majority of the time.

Sometimes the unexpected has worked in my favor. Through a series of weird events, I ended up in radio and television, even though radio/ television wasn't my degree plan. At all. My degrees are in psychology and literature. I ended up on a highly coveted morning show in radio, and from that position was hired away into television news, while people who attended the same university I did but had actual degrees in radio and television didn't get those positions. Bizarre.

And then there were those things I prepared for and prayed for and aimed for and aspired to that didn't happen. I never thought I would end up living in Texas. I thought I would be living on a beach, running my psychology practice in a quaint seaside town and writing novels on the side. I also thought I might be in music. I figured I would get married at some point. And maybe in my late thirties I'd have a couple three kids. You know, that number? A couple three? It's a thing in my head.

Fast forward all these years, and my life's story is more fascinating, more beautiful, more challenging, and ever-growing, in far different ways than I ever could have imagined. Good thing my expectations didn't get their way when I consider what I would have missed.

**Where did you think you would live when you grew up? What kind of job did you see yourself in? Who were the kind of people you wanted in your life?**

Our Footnote this week is someone who, unknowingly, would become known for something far different from what he set out to become.

It's difficult to overstate what a major player Quirinius (pronounced kwi-RIN-i-us)[1] was in the Roman scheme of things. His full name was Publius Sulpicius Quirinius, and he was born in 51 BC in a small town outside of Rome. He was born into an aristocratic family, which, in Roman times, meant that his family had achieved position and power through generations of outstanding military achievement on behalf of Roman emperors. But it was through his ambition and drive that he achieved far more than his illustrious ancestors. He used his military achievements to ultimately make his way into the complex world of Roman politics, a climber who didn't rest on his family's military background but smartly used the benefits of his family name to leverage even greater glory.

When you dig back through annals of history, you find all kinds of fascinating achievements of Quirinius. He won decisive battles. He was highly valued by Augustus, the first emperor of the Roman Empire—that legend who battled Mark Antony and Cleopatra. Augustus would ultimately be known as one of the most powerful and successful leaders of Rome, and our guy Quirinius was all up in the middle of that achievement and expansion. So trusted was Quirinius by Augustus that Augustus appointed him the tutor for his grandson Gaius Caesar. Quirinius knew how to play the game. He moved his allegiances to whomever he needed to for maximum networking advantage. He married a girl with the right pedigree, then divorced her when a more popular woman became available. He had the right education, the right mentor, the right standing.[2]

But we don't study about him in history. We don't remember him for all the things he was striving to be remembered for. As we see in this week's video, we recall his name only because of the role he served in getting Mary and Joseph to Bethlehem for the census, so that Scripture would be fulfilled.

**Look up Micah 5:2 and write it below.**

We believe the Book of Micah in the Old Testament was written at some point between 742 and 687 BC.[3] This means that this particular prophecy was recorded a good seven hundred years before Quirinius would call for his census over the Judean province for which he served as governor. And that also means that this prophecy was right as Rome was being founded as a city by Romulus as stated in Roman tradition, a small enclave of farmers sprinkled amongst the seven hills along the banks of the Tiber.

*He has made everything beautiful in its time. He has also set eternity in the human heart; yet no one can fathom what God has done from beginning to end.*
*Ecclesiastes 3:11*

**What does this information tell you about the planning nature of God? What does it tell you about how He may likely view time and history and how long things take?**

**Read Ecclesiastes 3:11 in the margin (we'll be spending some time in Ecclesiastes over our days together this week). What do**

we learn from this verse about God and His relationship with time?

**Now read 2 Peter 3:8-9 in the margin. How does God's concept of time differ from yours?**

For many years, every little town and burg had its own "time" based on the position of the sun to that particular town. Through sundials and other means, people living in communities would experience their own "time." But when railroads were developed, those means of keeping local time made for a scheduling disaster in making sure passengers were ready to board or disembark. There actually became something known as "railway time," and there were watches developed that showed both the local time of a town and the railway time, which was what the train schedule was run off of with its more standardized way of considering the clock. In 1883, there was finally the official adoption of national standardized time zones, insisted upon by the American railroad system.[4] 1883! How crazy is that? We've been operating off the same clock in this country for only the last 136 years or so!

In our lives, we can too often be out of sync with the "railway time" of God's rendering of time.

**Has there been a season in your life in which it seemed God would never "arrive" with what you were praying for and hoping for? Did He ultimately arrive? What was that like, navigating the gap between your expectation and when things actually came to be?**

Sometimes God shows up with something far earlier than we expected and we can feel unprepared and unready for our next assignment. But as we will see in the next lesson, God is always right on time.

## 2

*The truth is of course that what one calls the interruptions*
*are precisely one's real life.*

C. S. Lewis, *Thee Letters of C. S. Lewis to Arthur Greeves*

### But We Had a Plan

My husband, Mike, has an easy, winning nature. He genuinely, genuinely, genuinely likes people . . . and people usually like him back. He's a great communicator, an effective debater, and a confirmed government and politics geek (and a soccer nerd—but that's another story). He was the guy who was always in student government and was class president many times throughout the years. While still in college, he worked for state representatives, a U.S. congressman, and a U.S. senator. The obvious plan was to head to law school, pass the bar exam, start at the state level, and run for office. At a very young age, he had the plan mapped out, strategies and education procured, gleaming career in his sights, with backers and politicos cheering him on.

But life intervened.

A university campaign his senior year turned into a mess.

The law school scholarship was smaller than we'd hoped. Much smaller.

And our ten-year plan for our early marriage got turned upside down by a positive pregnancy test seven months after our nuptials.

The blooming political career was put on hiatus while we scrambled to deal with real life and to provide for our new daughter. After a while, the dreams and plans for Mike's political career were placed on a shelf, dust gathering on the gilded edges. By his late twenties, Mike felt that he had failed. He had a full-on midlife crisis, having placed his identity in a future political career. And it didn't help that many others had placed those expectations on him as well.

Sometimes in life, we try and we flat-out fail. Other times we do our best, but things just don't happen as we expect or hope they will.

**Have you ever confused something not happening in your life with failure? If so, what was it?**

**What is something in your life that is far different from what you had planned? Is it where you live? what your career is or isn't? your family life?**

**What if you recast something you see as a failure into something you see as part of your story, something powerful to tell? How would that change your perspective on certain events in your life?**

What do we do when it all turns out different than we imagined? Who are we in that scenario? How do we deal with the confusion of it all? Blithe platitudes do little good. Smug assurances that it will all work out ring hollow. Because our culture puts such emphasis on work, on career, it can be a core hurt, a deep bewilderment when it goes awry. And it's not just the business world of which I speak. It includes those who have longed for a career as a parent or as a spouse.

There's the script we write. And then there's the script God writes. Some elements will match up. Others won't.

The smartest guy who ever lived had a few things to say about work and career. Look up Ecclesiastes 3:22 and write down what King Solomon had to say on the topic.

The first part of the verse reads a little like an inspirational poster (ever have one of those?), but the second part of the verse brings a bit of perspective back into the conversation. What are your impressions on Solomon's thoughts?

Now check out Ecclesiastes 6:3-6. What strikes you about these verses? What do they say to you about finding a proper fulfillment in work and life?

In Christian circles we can encounter all kinds of attitudes and perspectives on work and career—both derogatory and encouraging. Some emphasize home and family while others talk of provision and opportunity and dreams. And some seem ambivalent or even apathetic at times.

Look up 2 Thessalonians 3:6-13 and see what Paul has to say about apathy or idleness.

When it comes to your career or work or vocation, where do you need to trust God more? Where do you need to realign your true identity?

What kind of emphasis do you think our culture places on career?

How much self-identity do you place in your career/work/vocation?

How much of your thought-life real estate is claimed by thoughts of your work?

I've often thought of what I'm achieving in my work as the "thing" I'll be remembered for. I've often viewed my worth, my value, through the lens of my work. For some of us, what we achieve in our careers might just be the thing we're remembered for. But we actually don't get to control that once we're gone, which elicits an important reminder for me: I want to make sure I'm keeping an appropriate watch on my motivations for what I'm doing and how well it balances with other important components and responsibilities in my life.

## Who Would've Thought?

On a busy highway at the corner of a stoplight into a beautiful West Austin neighborhood sits a cluster of old cabins nestled under a bank of trees. I've passed by it so many times but, until recently, never took the time to figure out what it was. Turns out it's the Bowles's family settlement. A placard at the site tells the story.

Dietrich Bowles showed up in this area, west of Austin, in the 1850s. He thought the city of Austin was getting too busy and crowded. (Can you imagine what he would think of this city now?) At the time, the land he chose was about a day's travel from Austin's bustling population of 900, and Bowles decided this was the spot to build a family enclave. His remote family settlement site is now one of the highest growth areas of the Austin Metro region. Tens of thousands of cars go zipping by the family settlement every day. Real estate values are through the roof. Dietrich may have thought that the land he was taming and the cabins he was building would long sit outside the craziness and bustle of an urban area. But one hundred fifty years later, it's smack in the middle of a metro population of over two million people.

Our intentions don't always turn out the way we envision, just like that Footnote of ours, Quirinius, who seemed to think he would be remembered for his brilliant military and political career.

**Are you a personality who likes to be in control, who likes for things to go as planned? If so, describe the emotions that show up when life takes a different turn.**

**What fears arise when things seem to spiral far from the way you thought they would be?**

At the end of the day, for many of us, the idea that we won't accomplish what we want to in this life, that time will run out before we've had a chance to "make our mark," leaves us queasy. In a riff on philosopher René Descartes's famous saying "*Cogito, ergo sum*" ("I think, therefore I am"), we often define our existence by being known by those around us and by believing that we will be remembered after we are gone, making our saying, "I am known by people, therefore I am." And just like we talked about last week in our study of Epaphras, there are certainly things I want to be known for, that I want to be intentional about.

But I'm reminded that there will come a day, that, for most of us, no matter what we've achieved, no matter how intentional we've been, no matter how strategic and smart we were in our career or life choices, those who might remember us will also be gone.

Part of what I love about writing and researching is all the bunny trails I come across, all the odd places I go trekking in the pursuit of a little crumb of trivia that makes a big point, the hunt for new insights and the connection of things that don't seem related. For this study, I went down one of those bunny trails as I was researching our first Footnote, Tychicus. If you'll remember, I mentioned my paternal great-great-grandmother and her maiden name of Bridges. Now, girls, I could have stopped there. But, with a deadline looming for this project and more items on a to-do list that always seems endless, it seemed like the right moment to take a deep Google dive into more of my genealogy on my dad's side. (Please tell me I'm not the only one who does this, who decides an obscure internet search trumps all other immediate tasks.)

The last time I had done an internet search on my dad's family, I'd only been able to get back to around the time of that great-great-grandmother Jennie Bridges Lyles of mine, but this time some of my relatives had chased more of the records and had been able to trace things way back. *Way* back. And I found myself, late into the night, contacts burning themselves onto my tired eyeballs, peering at the name of my thirteen-generations-back ancestor, John Lyles. I was able to find the little village where he was born in the mid-1500s in a tiny remote village in northern England. It was exhilarating.

And it was sobering. Because all I have at this point, probably all I will ever have in this life, is his name. Not his favorite color. Not his favorite food. Not his profession. Not what he worried about. Not if he felt like he lived up to all he aspired to in life. The paper trail ends with only his name. And I realized, if God continues to allow this world to spin for another five hundred years, then maybe, just maybe, a future descendant of mine might take it upon himself or herself to do a late-night database search for me. But it will never make me completely known to them.

God is the only one who can fully know and love us.

**Understanding that there will likely come a day when we are no longer remembered on this planet, what does that say to you about where you want to invest your time and heart?**

**Read Matthew 6:19-21 in the margin. What do you think Jesus means by "treasures on earth"? Do you think He was referring only to material possessions, or could it also include human accolades and positions?**

**Perhaps you're someone who takes life as it comes, not worrying too much about what's around the corner. But there is a "future you" out there who needs some attention. What kind of treasures do you want to store up in heaven, and what kind of person do you need to be in order to have that kind of focus? What could that mean for who you will be by the end of this year? In five years?**

It's a tough pill to swallow, I know, but there will probably be a day when our great-great-great-great-grandkids don't know our names, or that church where we've spent so much time serving has no plaque recording our contributions, or that project we invested so much time in gets replaced by something newer and better and faster. But keeping that future anonymity in mind is good medicine for me and for you. It helps cure us of a possible arrogance about the future and can create a good gut check for our today.

# 3

*It is not your business to succeed, but to do right;*
*when you have done so, the rest lies with God.*

C. S. Lewis, *Yours, Jack: Spiritual Direction from C.S. Lewis* (2008)

## Better Than He Aspired to Be

I experienced a truly unusual childhood, one that I had no idea at the time was unusual. My dad, Bob Lyles, was a rocket scientist. Not even kidding. An actual rocket scientist. So although people say, "Well, it's not rocket science," it actually was at my house. The reason it didn't seem all that unusual to me was because I was growing up in it. And so many of my friends in the same community had parents who were also involved in the rocket industry, in space flight, as their careers. My brother's soccer coach on Saturday afternoons was also the guy who, on Monday morning, flew the 747 with the space shuttle piggybacked on top of it from Edwards Air Force Base out to Cape Canaveral. You know, the usual.

My dad had big aspirations. He'd been raised as the kid of two sweet sharecroppers in rural Mississippi. Their integrity and work ethic were always evident in his personal morale, but he longed for bigger and higher things, literally. He saw the burgeoning space exploration industry beginning to bloom during his early college years and set his sights on the stars. He put in the time, the hard work, the effort, the networking.

But at what should have been the zenith of his career, twenty years later, when he had two decades of solid experience and reputation behind him, the corner office suite, and a couple more decades dawning in a bright horizon of opportunity, he awoke one morning unable to move. A nagging stiff neck and a history of irritating back issues suddenly converged into a huge medical emergency and he found himself undergoing a dangerous and risky surgery to try to restore movement and function to his powerful, tall form. Several years of further surgeries and experimental procedures followed, along with visits to some of the most influential medical organizations in the U.S., including the Mayo Clinic.

We never did receive a completely clear diagnosis for what was going on with him medically. We obviously remained concerned about his physical condition, but it was for his soul that we worried the most. He was such a driven man, with such high goals. From the time I was a child, he would have my brothers and me list our goals for the week on a 3x5 index card and show it to him on a Monday, knowing that he expected us to have momentum on those items by Friday. This was when I was in the third and fourth and fifth grades, y'all. My primary goals in those ages and stages were to somehow worm my way into the popular crowd and to not get beat up at the bus stop again. But still, my dad wanted to see those goals cataloged on those cards.

For someone with that kind of drive, who had pushed himself from the farm of his youth to the sparkling streams of science and success in the space race, for that kind of a person to be confronted with taking early disability from his career was devastating. What would his legacy be now? What would he be known for?

He had wanted to have enough financial success in his lifetime to gift a university with a building, a place where people could engage in further scientific research. He had huge philanthropic goals that were now sidelined. He had seasons of feeling a great loss, a significant grief that life had shifted so abruptly. He ignored God for a while, not at all sure God existed. Then he got good and mad at God. Then he made his peace with God and dove into reading more of the Bible and the deep math and quantum he found there.

Little did he know, but through all of that, he was building an incredible legacy. He wrote three books to keep his active mind growing and engaged. He built complex deck systems for the houses he and my mother lived in, one at the base of the Wasatch mountains, one in the high desert of Arizona, and one at their final home in Oklahoma, where they moved to be closer to grandchildren. And he built those decks while navigating with a cane or while in what he called his "scooter," a motorized wheelchair. He built rocket models out of Legos with the grandkids. He made documentaries and narrated them on his computer, so that his grandchildren would know his perspective on what those years in the rocket industry were like. He fought and he questioned and he researched and he stretched and he tried and he just. kept. on.

His grandchildren find it to be a cool anecdote that some of his rocketry work is on display in museums and on certain space systems still today. But that's not what they remember him for. They remember a compelling and kind man. They remember a mind that turned and spun every box on its axis. They remember a consummate problem solver. They remember the innovations he came up with to make his life more effective when this mysterious spinal issue felled him.

I remember him as the man who stood above everyone else at almost six and a half feet tall, his height cut in half when he had to spend his last several years in a wheelchair. But, for his grandchildren, his height didn't matter. To them, he was, and is, a giant. Not because of his career. But because of what he brought to his life's challenges. Because of what he invested in them. Because of their conversations. Because of the tomatoes they planted together. Because of the way he taught them to use tools. Because of the questions he asked them.

He wanted to leave them a legacy of his accomplishments. But the accomplishments that he is truly known for now live beyond a space shuttle program that, at this point, has literally been resigned to the mothballs in our nation's history.

**What kind of expectations were placed on you as a child when it came to behavior and education? Were you raised in a high-expectations climate? How did you respond to that?**

**Many of us either try to reach the expectations placed on us in childhood, or we rebel against them. What have you seen in your own life, in the lives of your friends, your spouse, when it comes to their responses to the expectations of their childhoods?**

*What do people get for all the toil and anxious striving with which they labor under the sun?*

*Ecclesiastes 2:22*

**Read all of Ecclesiastes 2. And if possible, read it fully in a couple of different versions. (I recommend the New International Version and *The Message*. You can access both versions on any online Bible website.)**

**Read Ecclesiastes 2:22 in the margin. Circle the word *striving*.**

*Striving* is an interesting word when we look at the etymology of it. (Etymology is the study of where words came from, or the cultures and languages from which words originated.) The English language comprises about 30 percent French; 30 percent Latin; 24 percent Germanic languages (including Old Norse and Old English words); a little over 5 percent Greek; about 4 percent Spanish, Portuguese, and Italian; and a little over 3 percent from the proper names of things, such as your first name and mine.[5]

Because of all those influences on our language, we sometimes lose important nuances and intentions of original words, and that's where my love of etymology comes in. When I dig back into a word's origins, I'm fascinated at what I find. There is a great online tool for finding word origins called etymonline.com, and it's there that we discover that *strive*, the origin of the word you circled above, has more layers to it than we typically think of.

When I think of *strive* in my modern context, I tend to think of it as working hard toward something, of giving that extra push. Of hustle and every meme that comes with that. But *strive* is an old word in French, from *estriver*, and it means to "quarrel, dispute, resist, struggle, put up a fight, compete."[6] When I read this definition, I realize that when I find myself striving to reach my own aspirations or goals, what I am really doing is fighting for my place in history—in significance, in reputation, in achievement. And maybe, just maybe, I shouldn't be fighting and quarreling and competing for these things at all.

**Is there something you have been striving for?**

What does Solomon say to us in Ecclesiastes 2:22–23 about many of the things we strive for?

What are some things you strived for in high school or college? How do those things affect you even today?

Think about something you desperately wanted in your young adult life that you didn't get—a position, a romantic relationship, a certain apartment or house or car. What impact did that have on you moving forward? (And please note, this isn't an attempt to minimize something that was important to you that didn't happen. There are absolutely things that we strive for and don't get that have a massive impact on our lives.)

From that experience, what did you learn? How did it possibly change your course or direction?

## Career and Title Don't Belong to Us Anyway

For some of you, being a wife and mother was what you dreamed of as a little girl. And I want to take a moment and put a stake in the

ground here: to have the dream of being a wife and mom is amazing. If that's all you have ever wanted, don't ever let a hurry-and-hustle world tell you it doesn't measure up in today's culture. And if you're someone who wanted a husband and kids but also wanted to work away from the house, that's amazing as well. There are examples all through Scripture of women who lived in both of those lanes and did it with passion and excellence. Let's put to rest once and for all this strange competitiveness around women's dreams and the inclination to evaluate some as more "noble" than others. Okay? Alright? Alright. Soapbox over, for the moment.

So let's say you wanted to become a wife and mom and stay home with your kids from the get-go. And let's say you've gotten to do that, are in the middle of doing that. You and your husband stayed in that tiny apartment longer so you could live off one income. You made major adjustments to your budget to accomplish your goal of being your children's primary caregiver during the day. You did all the things; you are achieving what you set out to do.

But what next? And I don't ask this to throw cold water on this beautiful season in your life. I ask it because I've seen far too often women who get sideswiped when the clock keeps ticking and the calendar keeps flipping and all of a sudden they find themselves with two kids in college and the third about to graduate from high school. We call it "empty nest syndrome" in our culture, and it is a real thing. I've seen women struggle wildly because their identity was so wrapped in their role as a mom that they didn't see the day coming when that role would morph and change.

I love my role as the women's ministry lead at my home church. It's a position I've had almost since the church began. I'm thankful for the experience of watching the church grow from a couple hundred people, with a handful of women attending my one Bible study, to a thriving faith community of multiple campuses, thousands of people, and a women's ministry program that has grown and grown and grown some more. I like my position. I like being known. I like the behind-the-scenes experiences. I like the access I have to many of the special guests, musicians, and speakers we host at our events. I like being known by my title within our congregation.

But here's the thing. None of it is really mine. Not the title. Not the access. Not the responsibilities. Not the privileges. I'm engaged in them. I have a duty to them. I enjoy them. But I've got to make sure I don't allow those things to become *me*. Because they aren't.

Every role we occupy, every desk we sit at, every season we are engaged in, is transitory.

**Look up John 21:18. What does Jesus tell the apostle Peter?**

I don't bring this verse up to discourage us. John goes on to explain that Jesus utters these words to Peter to foretell how Peter would die. And, indeed, tradition reports that Peter was crucified upside down in Rome, his inverted execution his final statement about his deference to Jesus—that in light of the holiness of Christ he did not find himself worthy of being crucified in the same position. I bring this verse up because, even though these words were spoken over Peter prior to Jesus's death and resurrection in a time when there didn't seem to be much benefit to following Jesus, Peter would go on after Christ's ascension to lead the early church. He would go on to become a man of considerable power and influence over the growing number of young Christians. His words to the church would make their way into Scripture. He would hold the highest position in the new church, that of bishop of the church at Rome, and would be called by later church leaders the Prince of the Apostles. The historian Jerome records that Peter held that position for twenty-five years.[7]

But that high position? That influence? That policy making? That leadership position? It didn't last for Peter. Years went by. Christianity was seen as more and more of a threat. And when Nero, the Roman emperor, decided that he was done with the gaining influence of the Christian church, he had Peter arrested and thrown into a Roman prison. Peter was ultimately executed, probably around the time of the Great Fire of Rome of AD 64. And in that, Peter fulfilled the prophecy Jesus had spoken to him all those years before: "'Very truly I tell you, when you were younger you dressed yourself and went where you wanted; but when you are old you will stretch out your hands, and someone else will dress you and lead you where you do not want to go.' Jesus said this to indicate the kind of death by which Peter would glorify God" (John 21:18-19). From the very early stages of Peter's church "career," he knew that on the horizon was a time that he would lay down the power and influence of that position and submit to a death that would glorify God and be catalytic in the spread of Christianity.

There are no gold watches when it comes to Christian retirement. Actually, there is no Christian retirement. We move from glory to glory, as Paul says in 2 Corinthians 3:18, all the days of our journey with Jesus. And at the end, instead of a gold watch, there is a crown not of gold but of life to welcome us home (James 1:12).

Through the laying down of his successful fishing business to going to Rome to evangelize to the city, to organizing and leading the young church, to ultimately being taken from that role and moving into the role of prisoner, Peter remained the one thing that circumstances could neither give him nor take away from him: a follower of Jesus. That was where his true identity was secure. His life was "hidden with Christ in God" (Colossians 3:3).

**How challenging do you find it to release certain roles in your life?**

**What are some roles that have recently ended for you? What in your life has transitioned? What are the strangest parts of adjusting to this new season?**

I lost my precious in-laws in quick succession over two years. While I still identify as their daughter-in-law, I am no longer functionally a daughter-in-law. No responsibility to send them cards on Mother's Day and Father's Day. No kids' school pictures to update for them. It's a very weird transition. We can have transitions in our everyday roles as well as in our spiritual roles.

**What do you think of as your "place" in your faith community? How much of your faith hinges on that identity?**

**What helps you make sure you are walking with Jesus for His reputation or renown and not for yours (for example, Scripture verses, specific questions or thoughts, practices, and so on)?**

Ah, Quirinius. Little did you know that we would recall your name centuries later only because of a King you never saw coming. You thought you were making all the right moves in your career. Instead, it was God moving you right where He wanted you so that prophecy would be filled.

My sisters. Little did you know that your name will be recalled by a Father who loves you and has known you from the beginning. You may go down as a legend for generations that follow. You may not. On your deathbed, you may feel you accomplished everything you set out to do. You may feel as though there is still much that needed to be done. Either way, God has you right where He needs you.

**As we close our time together, read Hebrews 6:10. What promise do you find there?**

God will not forget you. You might be a Footnote, but you are essential to the story—His story.

Because, this: "You show that you are a letter from Christ, the result of our ministry, written not with ink but with the Spirit of the living God, not on tablets of stone but on tablets of human hearts" (2 Corinthians 3:3).

It's a better story. It's an eternal one, not a script that will get lost in the crush of the ages.

For some of us, the twists and turns of life and our legacy will be one of the deepest places we have to trust God. It will be the area of our greatest surrender. But this: "God had planned something better for us so that only together with us would they be made perfect" (Hebrews 11:40).

God, edit our lives.

Help us let You do it.

Write Your story.

## The Careerist

*We can trust in God's plan for our lives in His greater story.*

### Welcome/Prayer/Icebreaker (5-10 minutes)

Welcome to Session 4 of *Footnotes*! This week we're exploring what Quirinius has to teach us about what it means to entrust our lives and our legacies to God and His plan. Take a moment to open with prayer, and then go around the circle and share about a career or life ambition you had as a child.

### Video (about 20 minutes)

Play the "Getting Started: A Devotional Reflection" video (optional), taking a couple of minutes to focus your hearts and minds on God's Word. Then play the video segment for Session 4, filling in the main idea as you watch and making notes about anything that resonates with you or that you want to be sure to remember.

---

### —Video Notes—

**Scripture:** Luke 2:1-3

**Main Ideas:** Your secular job can absolutely result in _____ _____.
At the end of the story, God ultimately is the _____.

**Other Insights:**

---

## Group Discussion (20-25 minutes for a 60-minute session; 30-35 minutes for a 90-minute session)

### Video Discussion

- What does it mean to walk with God even when you don't know what He's up to? Where in your life is God leading you to move and grow but you don't know why or where this will all end up?

### Workbook Discussion

- Read aloud Ecclesiastes 3:11 and 2 Peter 3:8-9. What do we learn from these verses about God and His relationship with time? (page 90–91) How does God's concept of time differ from ours?
- Has there been a season in your life in which it seemed God would never "arrive" with what you were praying for and hoping for? Did He ultimately arrive? What was that like, navigating the gap between your expectation and when things actually came to be? (page 91)
- Has your education and career path turned out exactly as you planned? What are some of the job and career changes you've had in your life? What did you learn from the experiences?
- Do you come from a long line of people who felt their legacies would be their careers or accomplishments? How has that impacted the decisions you have made in your life?
- Read aloud Ecclesiastes 2:22. Do you think it is wrong to be ambitious? How can you view ambition through the lens of what it means to *strive* (as we explored on page 102)? Is it possible to have healthy ambition?
- How do you keep your identity as a child of God first, over the titles, the distinctions, the achievement of your work or accomplishments (whether outside or inside the home)? Do you have a healthy view of the work you do, whether you love it or hate it? How have you let it define you?
- If you could bend time and go back and visit your twenty-year-old self, what would today's you tell the younger you about work/career or vocation?
- Understanding that there will come a day when we are no longer remembered on this planet, what does that say to you about where you want to invest your time and heart?
- How would you describe your life's calling? How do you find fulfillment in the roles and responsibilities you have as part of this calling or vocation?

**One to One (10-15 minutes, 90-minute session only)**

Before dividing up into groups of 2-3, play the "A Final Word" segment for the full group. Then divide into small groups and discuss the following:

- How have you been affected by realizing the powerful significance of four people you may have considered insignificant before?

- How does this realization change the way you see your own life within the context of God's story?

- What in your life could you mark with the hashtag #littlethingsarebigthings in a new way?

**Closing Prayer (5 minutes)**

Close the session by sharing personal prayer requests and praying together. In addition to praying out loud for one another, ask God to help you allow Him to edit the story of your life, knowing that He sees the bigger picture and is working all things for good.

# Leader Helps

## Tips for Facilitating a Group

### Important Information

Before the first session you will want to distribute copies of this study guide to the members of your group. Be sure to communicate that, if possible, they are to complete the first week in the study guide *before* your first group session.

For each week there are personal lessons divided into three sections, which participants may choose to complete in three sittings or all at once depending on their schedules and preferences.

As you gather each week with the members of your group, you will have the opportunity to watch a video, discuss and respond to what you're learning, and pray together. You will need access to a television and DVD player with working remotes. Use the Group Session Guide at the end of each week's lessons to facilitate the session (options are provided for both a 60-minute and a 90-minute format). In addition to these guides, the Group Session Guide Leader Notes (pages 116–20) provide additional helps including a Main Objective, Key Scripture reference, and Footnote Overview for each session.

Creating a warm and inviting atmosphere will help make the women feel welcome. You might consider providing snacks for your first meeting and inviting group members to rotate in bringing refreshments each week.

As group leader, your role is to guide and encourage the women on the journey to discovering that their lives matter in God's great story. Pray that God would pour out His Spirit on your time together, that the Spirit would speak into each woman's life and circumstances, and that your group would grow in community together.

## Preparing for the Sessions

- Be sure to communicate dates and times to participants in advance.
- Be sure that group members have their workbooks at least one week before your first session and instruct them to complete the first week of personal lessons in the study guide. If you have the phone numbers or email addresses of your group members, send out a reminder and a welcome.
- Check out your meeting space before each group session. Make sure the room is ready. Do you have enough chairs? Do you have the equipment and supplies you need? (See the list of materials that follows.)
- Pray for your group and each group member by name. Ask God to work in the life of every woman in your group.
- Read and complete the week's readings in this study guide and review the group session guide. Select the discussion points and questions you want to make sure to cover and make some notes in the margins to share in your discussion time.

## Leading the Sessions

- Personally welcome and greet each woman as she arrives. Take attendance if desired.
- In order to create a warm, welcoming environment as the women are gathering, consider lighting one or more candles, providing coffee or other refreshments, and/or playing worship music. (Bring an iPod, smartphone, or tablet and a portable speaker if desired.) Be sure to provide name tags if the women do not know one another or you have new participants in your group.
- Always start on time. Honor the time of those who are on time.
- At the start of each session, ask the women to turn off or silence their cell phones.
- Communicate the importance of completing the weekly lessons and participating in group discussion.
- Encourage everyone to participate fully, but don't put anyone on the spot. Invite the women to share as they are comfortable. Be prepared to offer a personal example or answer if no one else responds at first.
- Facilitate but don't dominate. Remember that if you talk most

of the time, group members may tend to listen rather than to engage. Your task is to encourage conversation and keep the discussion moving.

- If someone monopolizes the conversation, kindly thank her for sharing and ask if anyone else has any insights.
- Try not to interrupt, judge, or minimize anyone's comments or input.
- Remember that you are not expected to be the expert or have all the answers. Acknowledge that all of you are on this journey together, with the Holy Spirit as your leader and guide. If issues or questions arise that you don't feel equipped to handle or answer, talk with the pastor or a staff member at your church.
- Don't rush to fill the silence. If no one speaks right away, it's okay to wait for someone to answer. After a moment, ask, "Would anyone be willing to share?" If no one responds, try asking the question again a different way—or offer a brief response and ask if anyone has anything to add.
- Encourage good discussion, but don't be timid about calling time on a particular question and moving ahead. Part of your responsibility is to keep the group on track. If you decide to spend extra time on a given question or activity, consider skipping or spending less time on another question or activity in order to stay on schedule.
- Do your best to end on time. If you are running over, give members the opportunity to leave if they need to. Then wrap up as quickly as you can.
- Thank the women for coming and let them know you're looking forward to seeing them next time.
- Be prepared for some women to want to hang out and talk at the end. If you need everyone to leave by a certain time, communicate this at the beginning of the group session. If you are meeting in a church during regularly scheduled activities, be aware of nursery closing times.

## Materials Needed

- *Footnotes* workbook
- *Footnotes* DVD and a DVD player
- Stick-on name tags and markers (optional)
- iPod, smartphone, or tablet, and portable speaker (if desired for gathering music)

## Group Session Guide Leader Notes

Use these notes for your own review and preparation. If desired, you can share the Main Objective, Key Scripture, and Footnote Overview with the group at the beginning of the session to set the tone for the session, as well as prepare everyone for content discussion, especially those who might have been unable to complete their personal lessons during the week.

### Session 1: Tychicus: The Bridge

MAIN OBJECTIVE

To see that we can become a connection for people to a loving God.

KEY SCRIPTURE

*Tychicus will tell you all the news about me. He is a dear brother, a faithful minister and fellow servant in the Lord. (Colossians 4:7)*

FOOTNOTE OVERVIEW

Throughout our study we will be examining minor characters in the Bible who teach us major lessons. We begin our study with Tychicus, who was Paul's communications director, so to speak. Tychicus (pronounced TIH-kih-kuhs[1]) traveled with Paul, connecting him with the various baby churches developing across Asia Minor. Tychicus helped Paul spread the gospel; though we don't know much else about his life or ministry, what we do know is that he was willing and eager to play his largely unseen but essential role in what God was doing at the time.

Tychicus challenges us to think about our own lives and the roles we are called to play. Though we tend to think those jobs "on the stage" are most important in sharing God's Word and purpose with others, often the most critical roles are more behind the scenes and far less public. Allowing God to use us—in whatever roles He places us in—can make a huge difference others' lives and point them to our generous, loving God.

God has put people in your life who need you as a bridge. They've come to a ridgeline in their lives. They may not even realize what they are looking for or know what God has on the horizon for them. What they do need is someone who is simply willing to connect them to God. Someone who is willing to invite them to the small group. Someone who is willing to listen to them when you chance to meet in the grocery store aisle. Someone who is willing to share a smile, extend a hand, be present with them. It's a responsibility placed on each of us, whatever our gifts and talents, whatever our calling. We can connect them to our loving God. We can be the bridges.

## Session 2: Joanna: *The Messenger*

### Main Objective

To see how we can serve as God's messengers by sharing what He has done for us and embracing what it means to *be* the church.

### Key Scriptures

*After this, Jesus traveled about from one town and village to another, proclaiming the good news of the kingdom of God. The Twelve were with him, and also some women who had been cured of evil spirits and diseases: Mary (called Magdalene) from whom seven demons had come out; Joanna the wife of Chuza, the manager of Herod's household; Susanna; and many others. These women were helping to support them out of their own means. (Luke 8:1-3)*

*On the first day of the week, very early in the morning, the women took the spices they had prepared and went to the tomb. They found the stone rolled away from the tomb, but when they entered, they did not find the body of the Lord Jesus. While they were wondering about this, suddenly two men in clothes that gleamed like lightning stood beside them. In their fright the women bowed down with their faces to the ground, but the men said to them, "Why do you look for the living among the dead? He is not here; he has risen! Remember how he told you, while he was still with you in Galilee: 'The Son of Man must be delivered over to the hands of sinners, be crucified and on the third day be raised again.'" Then they remembered his words.*

*When they came back from the tomb, they told all these things to the Eleven and to all the others. It was Mary Magdalene, Joanna, Mary the mother of James, and the others with them who told this to the apostles. But they did not believe the women, because their words seemed to them like nonsense. Peter, however, got up and ran to the tomb. Bending over, he saw the strips of linen lying by themselves, and he went away, wondering to himself what had happened. (Luke 24:1-12)*

### Footnote Overview

Our Footnote this week is a woman named Joanna, mentioned by name twice in the Gospel of Luke. She is described as the wife of Chuza, the "manager" or "steward" of Herod's household. What this meant was she had influence and resources, and we are told that she used those resources to support the ministry of the apostles. She was an early believer, one of a handful of women who saw Jesus's empty tomb and proclaimed the good news.

But what if Joanna and the girls had decided that they weren't qualified to let the apostles know about the empty tomb? What if she decided that she couldn't compromise her husband's important position by making such an outlandish claim? What if she had decided to leave the interpretation of that rolled-away stone to the "experts," the Roman officials who had overseen Jesus's execution, the Pharisees, and the sealing of the tomb? She would have missed out on having the honor of being one of the first to carry the message of the risen Christ.

What we can learn from Joanna is that we should use our words to proclaim the message of the gospel and that we can also use our resources (our time, our money, our talents) to further that message as well. That God gives each of us assignments of ways we can love those around us. May we receive them with open arms. Even when we feel ill-equipped. Even when we don't fully understand how to make it happen. Even when the world would tell us we're just women.

### Session 3: Epaphras: The Wrestler

MAIN OBJECTIVE

To understand that our commitment to prayer has lasting impact in the lives of others and for the church.

KEY SCRIPTURE

> *Epaphras, who is one of you and a servant of Christ Jesus, sends greetings. He is always wrestling in prayer for you, that you may stand firm in all the will of God, mature and fully assured. (Colossians 4:12)*

FOOTNOTE OVERVIEW

Epaphras (pronounced EP-a-fras)[2] was Paul's trusted friend, confidant, and ministry partner. He's mentioned only three times in Scripture, but we see painted there a picture of someone who was faithful, trusted, and passionate about serving the church. We learn that Epaphras wrestled in prayer. Paul doesn't just say Epaphras prayed. He doesn't just say Epaphras prayed a lot. Paul is very intentional to tell us the intensity Epaphras brought to praying, that he was "always wrestling" (Colossians 4:12). And Paul is clear that the prayers of Epaphras were specific, that the baby Christians in the church at Colossae would stand firm in the will of God.

What we learn about Epaphras, and glean from those quick words attributed to his memory, is what it means to wrestle in prayer, and what

we can learn not about the "how" of prayer but about the "why" that goes beyond us. We will discuss several obstacles to prayer, and how we can engage and overcome those obstacles. Though we may not always get answers or the answers we seek when we pray, we do receive fresh perspective. We may not always like the circumstances from which spring some of our most painful prayers, but we will receive peace. And we may struggle with continuing to pray over things that don't seem to be changing, but we develop perseverance in the doing.

All we know about Epaphras's prayer life is the most important thing we need to know—that he wrestled and grappled with and labored over those baby Christians in Colossae, not just for their immediate needs, but for the church that would be. It was what Epaphras was wrestling *for*, not the mechanics necessarily of how he was doing that. There is no one way to pray. The most important thing is that we do it. We can drop the stereotypes about what prayer looks like and embrace how God made us, discover what works for each of us, and get to it. Then we can watch things change!

## Session 4: Quirinius: The Careerist

MAIN OBJECTIVE

To realize that we can trust in God's plan for our lives in His greater story.

KEY SCRIPTURE

*In those days Caesar Augustus issued a decree that a census should be taken of the entire Roman world. (This was the first census that took place while Quirinius was governor of Syria.) And everyone went to their own town to register. (Luke 2:1-3)*

FOOTNOTE OVERVIEW

Our Footnote this week is someone who, unknowingly, became known for something far different from what he set out to become. Quirinius (pronounced kwi-RIN-i-us)[3] was a major player in the Roman scheme of things, who rose to be a trusted adviser of Augustus, the first emperor of the Roman Empire. Quirinius knew how to play the game. He moved his allegiances to whomever he needed to for maximum networking advantage. He married a girl with the right pedigree, then divorced her when a more popular woman became available. He had the right education, the right mentor, the right standing.

But we don't study about him in history. We don't remember him for all the things he was striving to be remembered for. We know his name only because of the role he served in getting Mary and Joseph to Bethlehem for the census, so that Scripture would be fulfilled.

Our intentions for our lives don't always turn out the way we envision. Quirinius, for example, seemed to think he would be remembered for his brilliant military and political career. Our aspirations and our work are important, but we must realize that our true identity is in God alone. Life will throw us all kinds of curveballs and hurl us into unexpected transitions, but through it all God holds our lives in His hands. When we trust that He knows what He is doing, we can rest and be secure in the knowledge that our legacy—whatever it is—serves a crucial part in His story.

# Video Notes: Answers

**Week 1**

Not all of us have to be in the driver's seat, but all of us can be a <u>bridge</u>.

**Week 2**

Ask not what the <u>church</u> can do for you; ask what <u>you</u> can do as the church.

**Week 3**

Are we willing in <u>diligence</u> and in <u>prayer</u>, like Epaphras, to wrestle . . . for those who come after?

**Week 4**

Your secular job can absolutely result in <u>Kingdom</u> <u>fulfillment</u>.
At the end of the story, God ultimately is the <u>editor</u>.

# Notes

## Week 1: Tychicus: The Bridge

1. "Tychicus," http://thebibleworkshop.com/tychicus-pronunciation/.
2. "honor," www.blueletterbible.org/lang/lexicon/lexicon.cfm?Strongs=G5092&t=NIV.
3. Kyle Webb, "Pennybacker Bridge," *Community Impact Newspaper*, March 11, 2014, https://communityimpact.com/austin/news/2014/03/11/pennybacker-bridge-2/.
4. "Percy Pennybacker," www.revolvy.com/page/Percy-Pennybacker.
5. Matthew Trost, "You asked Seth Godin absolutely anything—and he answered," TEDBlog, May 12, 2009, https://blog.ted.com/you_asked_seth/.
6. See www.precept.org/.

## Week 2: Joanna: The Messenger

1. Robin Ngo, "Tour Showcases Remains of Herod's Jerusalem Palace—Possible Site of the Trial of Jesus," Biblical Archaeology Society, March 20, 2018, www.biblical archaeology.org/daily/biblical-sites-places/biblical-archaeology-places/herods -jerusalem-palace-trial-of-jesus/.
2. Flavius Josephus, *The Wars of the Jews, or History of the Destruction of Jerusalem*, trans. William Whiston, book V, chap. 4, para. 4.
3. "Herod Antipas," www.newworldencyclopedia.org/entry/Herod_Antipas.
4. See www.2dance2dream.org.
5. See www.heartsforhearing.org/.

## Week 3: Epaphras: The Wrestler

1. Epaphras, *The New Westminster Dictionary of the Bible* (Philadelphia: Westminster, 1974), 269.

2. "hypomonē," www.blueletterbible.org/lang/lexicon/lexicon.cfm?Strongs=G5281&t=NIV; "paraklēsis," www.blueletterbible.org/lang/lexicon/lexicon.cfm?Strongs=G3874&t=NIV.

3. Joe Carter, "9 Things You Should Know About Prayer in the Bible," The Gospel Coalition, May 7, 2015, www.thegospelcoalition.org/article/9-things-you-should-know-about-prayer-in-the-bible1/.

4. W. Ross Rainey, "Epaphras, A Man of Prayer," Counsel Magazine, September 18, 2015, https://counselmagazineonline.com/articles/epaphras-a-man-of-prayer-colossians-17-8-412-13-philemon-23/.

## Week 4: Quirinius: The Careerist

1. "Quirinius," The New Westminster Dictionary of the Bible, 785.

2. "P. Sulpicius Quirinius," Livius.org, www.livius.org/articles/person/quirinius-p-sulpicius/.

3. "Micah," https://amazingbibletimeline.com/blog/micah/.

4. "Why Do We Have Time Zones?" www.timeanddate.com/time/time-zones-history.html.

5. "English language," https://simple.wikipedia.org/wiki/English_language.

6. "strive," Online Etymology Dictionary, www.etymonline.com/word/strive#etymonline_v_22189.

7. Saint Jerome, "De Viris Illustribus (On Illustrious Men)," New Advent, retrieved June 5, 2015, www.newadvent.org/fathers/2708.htm. "St. Peter, Prince of the Apostles," New Advent, www.newadvent.org/cathen/11744a.htm.

## Leader Helps

1. "Tychicus," http://thebibleworkshop.com/tychicus-pronunciation/.

2. "Epaphras," The New Westminster Dictionary of the Bible, 269.

3. "Quirinius," New Westminster Dictionary, 785.